For Bashes, Beaches, BBQs & Birthdays

DRINKS

W·I·T·H·O·U·T L·I·Q·U·O·R

by Jane Brandt

Illustrations by Jerry Joyner

Workman Publishing, New York

DEDICATION

For the Bishop, the carpenter, the carpetbagger, the cop, the handyman, the kids, the lawyer, and the secretary . . . they all know who they are.

ACKNOWLEDGMENTS

With special thanks and appreciation to Katherine Ness and Suzanne Rafer, who patiently and diligently edited these comments and recipes to assure the best degree of perfection possible, and to Jane and Billy Hitchcock who believed in me, and to Marion Glass who would have been so proud.

Library of Congress Cataloging in Publication Data

Brandt, Jane.
  Drinks without liquor.
  Includes index.
  1. Beverages. I. Title.
TX815.B83 1983   641.8'75   82-40504
ISBN 0-89480-358-1

Cover and book design: Wendy Palitz
Cover illustration: Jerry Joyner

Workman Publishing Company Inc.
1 West 39th Street
New York, NY 10018

Manufactured in the United States of America
First printing April 1983

10 9 8 7 6 5 4 3 2 1

CONTENTS

TO YOUR HEALTH

Even though I have found full ice cube trays in the fridge only seven times in twenty-two years . . . even though no one ever confessed to spilling anchovies in the chocolate syrup . . . and even though the kid who put play-dough in the blender still walks with a slight limp, the joys of raising a family of six children—now ranging from kinder-garten to college graduate—have been the richest ingredients of my life. Fueling and feeding this large family, liberally spiced with cats and dogs and lots of friends, is still a challenge.

Because I have always had one foot in the business world, and presently own and operate two secretarial services, my circle of friends and acquaintances is large and wide. Ideas for recipes have poured in from everyone. My children's thoughts and experiments are also a part of it.

I have found that being "busy" is never an excuse for not serving a most special drink to family or friends. This book has been assembled during the busiest days of my life, but they have been among the happiest too, and I am pleased to share these moments—all woven into my recipes.

So, Skål, Cheers, Bottoms Up, L'Chaym, Down the Hatch, To Your Health and Here's Looking at You Kid— but this time with a clear head. Toast in the New Year and continue throughout the seasons with a festive array of good-tasting, creative alternatives to alcoholic beverages. There are yummy shakes and ice cream floats for an anytime snack, sweet and fruity energizers to pick you up after a hectic morning, flavorful vegetable cocktails to serve before an elegant dinner, and enough creative concoctions to keep your party punch bowl popular.

Included too are low-calorie quenchers for the diet conscious, a whole slew of warming broths for cold winter days, and children's favorites for birthday celebrations, get-togethers, and sleepovers.

When unexpected family or friends drop in, when special party occasions arise, or when someone just wants something good to drink, *Drinks without Liquor* is ready to inspire you!

Ice

Ice blocks and rings melt slower than cubes, and they're especially good for those large-crowd punches.

❖ To make a plain ice block, simply use a container large enough to suit your need: plastic storage boxes are useful, or you can use a cake pan, an angel-food pan, or a loaf pan, even a mixing bowl for an extra-large block. Use ring or other shaped molds to add interest.

❖ To color an ice block or ring—for a St. Patrick's Day party or Valentine's Day brunch—just add food coloring to the water before freezing.

❖ To make it really festive, decorate the ice block, mold, or individual cubes: fill the container halfway with water and freeze it. Remove the container from the freezer, and arrange your decorations on the ice: flowers and greens, fresh fruit, even mini American flags for the Fourth of July. Then carefully add ½ inch of water and refreeze. When the decoration is set, fill the container the rest of the way, and freeze it thoroughly.

❖ To unmold an ice block or ring, dip the container briefly in a bowl of hot water. Slide the ice carefully into your punch bowl. If possible, put the ice in the bowl before you add the punch, to avoid overflows. If the punch is already in the bowl, go slowly!

❖ When crushing ice, never place whole cubes in your blender unless your instruction booklet says it's okay. If you aren't sure, put the cubes in a plastic bag first, then whack them with a mallet or hammer to break them into smaller pieces. Now add them to the blender, to complete the crushing.

USING THE RECIPES

I have given sugar quantities in these drinks according to my family's taste, but of course you may wish to adjust it to your own. If you like less sugar, try cutting the amount in half, and then add to it until the drink tastes right to you.

❖ In recipes that call for large quantities to be put through a blender, I have divided the amount into two batches to avoid any disastrous overflow. If in doubt, or if your blender is particularly small, you can always do the mixing in even smaller batches.

❖ In punches that have sherbet and soda as ingredients, you may find that a while after blending, the milky solids float to the top and the soda remains on the bottom. Just be sure you stir the punch a bit as you ladle it out.

ANTIDOTES FOR SPRING FEVER

Chase away spring fever with an energizing pick-me-up. Yogurt is just what the blender orders, easily combined with fresh fruit for what can only be described as a heavenly and, best of all, non-fattening drink.

Spring is also a time for family celebrations. Mothers and fathers have special days; Easter dinner awaits. Brides and grooms, showers for the mother-to-be, graduations and class reunions are all on the horizon and need an original and delicious beverage to accompany traditional cakes and treats.

Open the windows wide and welcome the return of the warm weather!

THE PRETTY MOMMA

This healthful combination of pineapple and apricot makes you feel good just looking at it—and the taste is divine.

1 20-ounce can crushed pineapple
1 cup apricot nectar
1 quart light cream
⅓ cup sugar
1 teaspoon grenadine syrup
Garnish: Pineapple cubes

Combine all the ingredients, through the grenadine syrup, in a blender and blend until smooth. Pour into 6 frosted glasses and garnish with pineapple cubes.

Servings: 6 tall glasses

FRUIT SHAKE

For the calorie conscious.

1 cup plain yogurt
½ cup honey
½ cup sliced fresh strawberries
½ cup diced fresh papaya
½ cup diced ripe cantaloupe
3 tablespoons raw sugar
2 tablespoons wheat germ
1 cup crushed ice
Garnish: Extra cantaloupe

1. Place all the ingredients, through the wheat germ, in a food processor or blender and process until smooth.

2. When the mixture is well blended, return half to the processor or blender, add the crushed ice, and process until thoroughly blended.

3. Add the iced mixture to the rest, stir well, and pour into frosted glasses. Garnish with the fruit slices.

Servings: 4 glasses

PINEAPPLE CARROT COCKTAIL

Low in calories, high in nutrition, and it goes especially well with a cottage cheese salad.

3 cups unsweetened pineapple juice
2 large carrots, cut into small pieces
½ teaspoon lemon juice
1 cup crushed ice

1. Place the pineapple juice, carrot pieces, and lemon juice in a blender and blend until liquefied.

2. Add crushed ice and blend again, until the ice is liquefied. Stir well.

3. Serve immediately.

Servings: 6 old-fashioned glasses

BILLY BOY'S APRICOT-YOGURT DRINK

An energizing pick-me-up, or perfect for a springtime breakfast eye-opener.

3 cups chopped fresh apricots, skins removed (about 1 pound), *or* drained canned apricots
4 tablespoons apricot preserves
4 cups plain yogurt
Cold milk as needed
Garnish: Wheat germ

1. Place the apricots and preserves in a food processor or blender and process until puréed, about 2 minutes. Pour the purée into a bowl.

2. Add the yogurt to the purée, beating with a wire whisk until fully incorporated.

3. Add just enough milk to the mixture to thin it slightly, but not too much or you'll lose the tangy apricot flavor. Refrigerate, covered, for about 1 hour.

4. Serve in mugs with a sprinkling of wheat germ on top.

Servings: 6 mugs

CUPBOARD KEEPERS: ... AND ADD PINEAPPLE JUICE

Pineapple juice can be used with a variety of other juices and sodas to make a quick and thirst-quenching drink. Add equal parts of one of the following:

Papaya juice
Ginger ale, 7-Up, or club soda
Orange juice
Apricot juice
Tea, strong and cold
Cranberry juice cocktail

HOT CELERY PICK-ME-UP

A nutritious substitute for lunch, and a definite change of pace for the calorie counter.

2 quarts beef stock, fresh or canned
4 to 6 large ribs celery with leaves, chopped
1 large carrot, chopped
2 leeks, well cleaned and finely chopped
¼ pound very lean ground beef
4 egg whites, beaten to a froth
½ teaspoon dried thyme
6 whole peppercorns
¼ teaspoon dried tarragon
Salt and pepper to taste
Garnish: Chopped celery leaves, chives, or parsley

1. Place the stock in a large saucepan and bring to a boil over medium heat. Add the celery, cover, and simmer for 30 minutes.

2. Put the carrot, leeks, and beef in a large saucepan. Gently stir in the beaten egg whites and the seasonings. Gradually add the hot stock, stirring constantly. Heat, stirring often, just to boiling. Reduce heat and simmer 20 minutes.

3. Place a sieve over a large mixing bowl, and gently ladle the mixture into the sieve, pressing the solids with the back of a wooden spoon to extract as much liquid as possible.

4. Serve in clear punch cups (or freeze in small containers for future use). Garnish with chopped celery leaves, chives, or parsley.

Servings: 8 punch cups

ELLEN'S ENERGIZER

Sassy stomach? This will help—and there's a low-calorie version too.

½ cup half and half *or* ½ cup skim milk

½ cup ginger ale *or* ½ cup low-calorie ginger ale

Pour the half and half over crushed ice in a tall glass. Add the ginger ale slowly, stirring constantly.

Servings: 1

THE SPORTSMAN

A high-protein milkshake, the perfect pick-me-up at any time of the day—or night. If you prefer, try 1 teaspoon maple syrup, frozen orange juice concentrate, or any fruit nectar in place of the molasses.

1 cup cold milk

1 teaspoon powdered brewer's yeast

2 tablespoons (or more) powdered skim milk

1 teaspoon molasses

Place all the ingredients in a blender and blend for 1 minute, until smooth. Serve immediately.

Servings: 1

ENERGY INNOVATION

Delicious even if you already feel energetic.

1 cup cold milk
½ cup vanilla yogurt
1 10-ounce package frozen raspberries, thawed
1 egg

Place all the ingredients in a blender and blend for 1 minute, until smooth. Serve in tall glasses.

Servings: 2 tall glasses

TED'S A.B.C.

Also excellent for a child's lunch box if you want to be sure of good nourishment during school days.

3 12-ounce cans chilled apricot nectar
2 bananas, sliced very thin
1 cup canned or fresh coconut milk (see page 18)
Garnish: Shredded coconut

Put half of each of the ingredients in a blender, and blend at high speed for 3 minutes. Pour the mixture into a bowl or pitcher and repeat with the other half of the ingredients. Stir the batches together and serve in frosted mugs with shredded coconut sprinkled on top.

Servings: 6 mugs

CAROLYN'S COCONUT CUTIE

If you have a sweet tooth as well as an eye for energy . . .

½ cup cold orange juice
½ cup plain yogurt
½ cup cream of coconut
¾ cup club soda
Garnish: 2 wafer-thin orange slices

1. Place the orange juice, yogurt, and cream of coconut in a blender, and blend for 1 minute.

2. Place 1 or 2 ice cubes in a tall frosted glass. Fill the glass halfway with the mixture, then gently add the club soda. Garnish each glass with an orange slice.

Servings: 2 tall glasses

COCONUT MILK COCKTAIL

Only one or two recipes in this book call for fresh coconut milk because grappling with a coconut is hard work. But the reward is worth it. Don't tackle this concoction without an ice pick and a hammer.

1 coconut
Garnish: Grated coconut and grated
  nutmeg

1. Preheat the oven to 300°F.

2. Puncture the eyes of the coconut with an ice pick (or long, sharp nail). Drain and reserve the "milk."

3. Bake the drained coconut, whole, for 15 minutes. Tap the shell with a hammer to open it. Remove the meat from the shell and chop it coarsely.

4. Blend equal amounts of coconut meat and warm water in a blender until evenly ground. Cool. Strain the coconut water through a sieve or cheesecloth into a bowl. Press hard to extract all the liquid. Add the reserved coconut milk. Cover and refrigerate.

5. If you wish to drink the coconut cocktail by itself, pour it into small glasses and sprinkle with grated coconut and/or nutmeg.

Servings: 6 small glasses

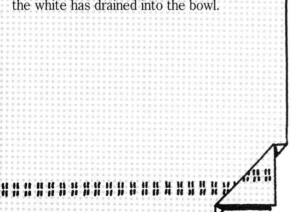

HOW TO SEPARATE AN EGG

Gently crack the shell by rapping it on the sharp edge of a bowl or cup, making sure the yolk doesn't break. Keep the yolk in one half of the shell and allow the white to run out into the bowl. Carefully transfer the yolk from one half to the other several times, until all the white has drained into the bowl.

THE PRAIRIE OYSTER

For the strong at heart: you swallow the egg yolk whole! (And it's guaranteed to cure a hangover.)

1 egg yolk (or 1 whole egg)
1 teaspoon Worcestershire sauce
2 dashes white vinegar
2 dashes Tabasco sauce
Pinch of salt and a grinding of pepper

Place the unbroken egg yolk (or whole egg) in a champagne glass and add the remaining ingredients. Then, down the hatch—good luck!

Servings: 1

SPINSTER'S POSSET

A posset was a substitute meal for invalids or people with sensitive stomachs. In olden days the milk was already warm, because it came straight from the cow. Although usually made with a bit of wine in order to curdle the milk, we have substituted a good "nip" of lemon juice.

1 quart milk
2 tablespoons fresh lemon juice (save the rind)
4 ounces sugar cubes
½ teaspoon ground ginger
¼ teaspoon grated nutmeg
Garnish: Extra grated nutmeg

1. Heat milk to just below boiling. Add the lemon juice (milk will curdle slightly), and remove from the heat.

2. Line a sieve with cheesecloth, place it over a medium-size bowl, and strain the milk through the sieve.

3. Rub the sugar cubes on the lemon rind.

4. Add sugar cubes, ginger, and nutmeg to the milk. Stir until the sugar dissolves.

5. Pour into punch cups, garnish with extra nutmeg, and serve hot.

Servings: 5 teacups

THE FARMER'S DAUGHTER

If you can't get fresh buttermilk, you can make the equivalent amount using powdered buttermilk concentrate, which can be found in most supermarkets.

1 quart buttermilk
1 pint lemon sherbet, softened
1 teaspoon sugar
Pinch of ground cinnamon

1. Place the buttermilk and sherbet in a mixing bowl and beat with a rotary beater or wire whisk until smooth.

2. Pour into tall frosted glasses and sprinkle each with a little sugar and cinnamon.

Servings: 4 tall glasses

RAINBOW BUTTERMILK

Pick a color for this nutritious drink, or make one of each—pink, lavender, yellow. (For individual drinks, use 1 cup of buttermilk to ½ cup of juice.)

3 cups buttermilk
1½ cups fruit juice (cherry, apricot, pineapple, peach, or grape)
1 tablespoon sugar, or to taste
Garnish: Grapes and fruit slices

1. Mix all the ingredients, through the sugar, in a pitcher and stir until the sugar dissolves.

2. Place several grapes in the bottom of each punch cup. Add the drink and top with a fruit slice.

Servings: 6 punch cups

THINK THIN COFFEE MILKSHAKE

No one will ever guess that this scrumptious shake contains only 85 calories.

1 cup cold skim milk
3 ice cubes, crushed
1 teaspoon powdered instant coffee
Artificial sweetener to taste

Place all the ingredients in a blender and blend until creamy.

Servings: 1

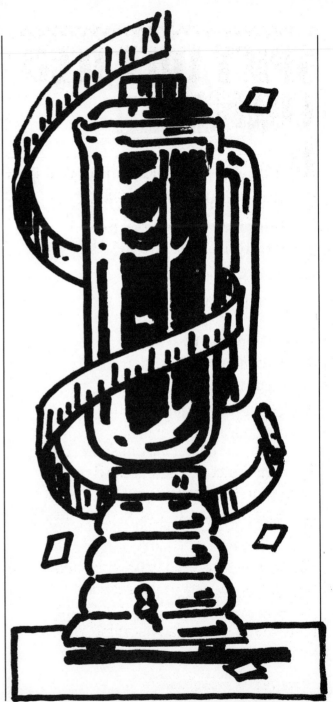

SPICY DIET ICED COFFEE

Drink this occasionally if you're counting those little calorie devils, or all summer long if you're just plain thirsty and love the taste of coffee.

3 cups strong hot coffee
1 cinnamon stick
3 whole cloves
½ teaspoon ground allspice
Artificial sweetener to taste
Garnish: Orange-peel strips

1. Pour the coffee into a bowl or pitcher and stir in the cinnamon stick, cloves, and allspice. Let it stand for 2 hours.

2. Remove the cinnamon stick and the cloves and serve over ice in tall glasses. Add artificial sweetener to taste and garnish each serving with a strip of orange peel.

Servings: 4 tall glasses

THE FRITZER

This diet cocktail is something like a spritzer—but not quite!

1 sugar cube, or 1 teaspoon sugar
2 dashes bitters
Lemon or orange peel
Club soda

Place the sugar in an old-fashioned glass and add the bitters, peel, and 2 or 3 ice cubes. Fill with club soda and stir.

Servings: 1 old-fashioned glass

THE ORAM

An exasperating drink for someone with a sweet tooth, but perfect for those who crave the unusual. This goes well with fresh Brie and other cheese appetizers.

2 cups tomato juice
2 cups sauerkraut juice
Strips of lemon rind
Tabasco sauce (optional)

Place the tomato and sauerkraut juices in a pitcher and stir well. Serve over crushed ice in cocktail glasses, adding a strip of lemon rind to each glass and, if you dare, a dash of Tabasco.

Servings: 8 cocktail glasses

SAUERKRAUT JUICE COCKTAIL

Learn to love the taste of sauerkraut by sipping this.

1 cup sauerkraut juice
Dash of onion powder
Juice of half a lemon

Thoroughly mix all the ingredients together and pour over crushed ice.

Servings: 1

STRAWBERRY (Not-So) ANGEL

This is really a luscious liquid parfait, so don't serve it with a heavy dessert—just some lacy cookies or a few slices of fresh fruit.

1 pint fresh strawberries, cleaned and chopped *or* 2 cups frozen strawberries and juice, thawed
1 13½-ounce can condensed milk
2 cups crushed ice
Garnish: Whole strawberries

Combine all the ingredients, through the ice, in a blender. Blend at high speed until smooth. Serve in punch cups or in tulip champagne glasses, with a strawberry on top.

Servings: 6 punch cups

STRAWBERRY SLIM

A pretty drink with a delicate taste and a delicate color. It's perfect for any time of the day.

2 cups fresh ripe strawberries
½ cup club soda
½ pint low-calorie vanilla ice cream *or* 1 8-ounce container of vanilla yogurt
½ cup skim milk
Garnish: Extra mint leaves

1. Wash and hull the strawberries.

2. Place all the ingredients, through the milk, in a blender and blend 1 minute until smooth.

3. Serve garnished with whole mint leaves.

Servings: 4 tall glasses

RAMBLING ROSE PUNCH

A refreshing and colorful addition to your Easter buffet table, this will complement a salty ham or a roast leg of lamb laden with garlic.

4 packages (10–12 ounces each) frozen
   strawberries, thawed
1 large can (12 ounces) frozen
   lemonade, thawed
Raspberry and mint ice mold
2 quarts ginger ale
Garnish: Wafer-thin orange slices

1. Place the berries and lemonade in a punch bowl and mix well.

2. When you are ready to serve, carefully add the ice mold to the mixture and pour in the ginger ale. Float orange slices on top.

3. Serve immediately.

Servings: 16 to 20 punch cups

THE CUKE

Toast the Easter Bunny with this, while passing a tray of cut-up raw vegetables. May be made in advance—it gains momentum in the refrigerator.

2 cups peeled, seeded, chopped
    cucumber
1 quart buttermilk
1 tablespoon finely chopped scallion
Salt and pepper to taste
Dash of garlic powder
1 tablespoon finely chopped parsley
Garnish: Wafer-thin cucumber slices
    (do not peel), paprika, and carrot
    curls

1. Put half of each of the ingredients, through the parsley, into a blender and blend for 1 minute until smooth. Pour the mixture into a large pitcher or a bowl, and repeat with the other half of the ingredients.

2. Combine the batches in the pitcher, mix well, and chill in the refrigerator for 2 hours.

3. Serve in punch cups, with a cucumber slice and a sprinkling of paprika on top.

Servings: 8 small punch cups

CURLING CARROTS

To make carrot curls, use a vegetable peeler to cut thin strips; wrap the strips around your finger and drop them into a bowl of ice water until you're ready to serve. The ice water will hold the curl in place.

BUGS BUNNY

This blender drink is delightful with ham salad made from the Easter-dinner leftovers. If you can force yourself to use skim milk instead of heavy cream, you will also have a zesty low-calorie companion.

1 large carrot, peeled and cut into small pieces
1 10½-ounce can concentrated chicken broth
2 cups heavy cream (or skim milk)
½ teaspoon celery salt
½ teaspoon onion salt
Freshly ground pepper to taste
Garnish: Carrot sticks topped with green olives

1. Place all the ingredients, through the pepper, in a blender and blend for 1 minute until smooth.

2. Pour the mixture into a medium-size saucepan and warm over low heat, stirring constantly.

3. When it is hot, serve immediately in punch cups garnished with an olive-topped carrot stick for a stirrer.

Servings: 8 punch cups

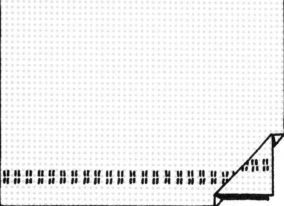

FROZEN FRUIT CUBES

Prepare peach, strawberry, pineapple, or watermelon cubes by cutting pieces of the fruit into ¾-inch chunks (fruit should be peeled, seeded, and cored first, if necessary). Dip each chunk into fresh lemon juice and place the cubes on a cookie sheet, not touching. Put the sheet in the freezer. When the fruit cubes are frozen solid, remove them and store them in a freezer bag. (These can also be used to cool any other beverage. They're pretty to look at, and they won't dilute the drink.)

SWEET SLUSH

These exciting beverages are easy to prepare once you have the frozen fruit cubes ready in advance.

2 cups frozen fruit cubes (see Frozen Fruit Cubes)
⅓ cup buttermilk or plain yogurt
3 teaspoons sugar
Garnish: Mint sprig

1. Put the frozen fruit cubes in a blender, but don't turn it on. Allow them to soften slightly, about 10 minutes.

2. Then add the buttermilk and sugar and blend well until smooth. Pour into a tall glass and add a sprig of mint.

Servings: 2 tall glasses

SAVORY LIME SLUSH

Use low-calorie ginger ale and sugar substitute, and you'll have a diet cooler.

2 cups frozen fruit cubes (see Frozen Fruit Cubes)
⅓ cup ginger ale
2 tablespoons fresh lime juice
1 tablespoon sugar
Garnish: Mint leaves or wafer-thin lime slice

1. Let the fruit cubes soften slightly in a blender, about 10 minutes.

2. Add the ginger ale, lime juice, and sugar. Blend until the mixture turns to slush, and serve immediately in a tall glass. Garnish with mint leaves or a slice of lime.

Servings: 1

KENTUCKY DERBY

A mock mint julep drink.

4 or 5 sprigs fresh mint
1½ cups sugar
2 cups cold water
¾ cup lemon juice (fresh, if possible)
1½ quarts ginger ale
Garnish: Wafer-thin lemon slices

1. Rinse the mint and discard the stems.

2. Place the sugar, water, and lemon juice in a medium-size bowl, mix, and stir in the mint leaves. Allow to stand for 30 minutes.

3. Fill a large pitcher with ice cubes, and strain the liquid over the ice. Add the ginger ale and lemon slices, and serve.

Servings: 10 tall glasses

THE MINT STINT

A marvelous, thirst-quenching treat for Kentucky Derby Day gatherings. Pass the peanuts!

2 6-ounce cans frozen lemonade concentrate, thawed
5 cups cold water
2 tablespoons finely chopped fresh mint leaves
Garnish: Wafer-thin lemon slices and mint sprigs

1. In a large pitcher, combine the lemonade with the water, stir, and add the chopped mint.

2. Fill tall glasses with ice cubes, add a lemon slice and a sprig of mint, and fill with the Mint Stint.

Servings: 6 tall glasses

A WORD ABOUT SPRING WATER AND MINERAL WATER

When a recipe calls for water you may, if you wish, substitute a mineral water or a natural sparkling water. Alone, with ice and a twist of lime, these spring waters have distinct flavors, depending upon their origin. They are pure, containing no calories and usually no salt.

If you live in an area where the water is heavily treated, you would definitely want to consider these spring waters to avoid the possibility of a medicinal or chlorine taste in your beverages.

STRAWBERRY PINEAPPLE SHAKER-UPPER

A real showstopper, but not for the scale hopper!

1 10-ounce package frozen strawberries, thawed
1 20-ounce can crushed pineapple
1 pint strawberry sherbet
1 pint vanilla ice cream
1 quart club soda
Garnish: Pineapple chunks

1. In halves, blend the strawberries, pineapple, sherbet, and ice cream in a blender at high speed for 1 minute. Pour into a large bowl and stir the batches together.

2. Fill each glass two-thirds full, then slowly add club soda to the top. Stir and serve, garnished with a pineapple chunk.

Servings: 6 tall glasses

BAPTIST WINE

This soothing drink can be made in any quantity. It's nicest served in wine glasses.

1 quart ginger ale, chilled
1 quart unsweetened grape juice, chilled

Mix ginger ale and juice in a pitcher or decanter, and serve in wine glasses.

Servings: 16 wine glasses

JUNE PUNCH

This is grand for any occasion. It goes well with tiny sandwiches or desserts and cakes.

6 cups extra-strong tea
2½ cups sugar
3 cups orange juice
2 cups unsweetened grapefruit juice
½ cup lime juice
½ cup lemon juice
Garnish: Mint sprigs and wafer-thin lemon slices

1. Place all the ingredients, through the lemon juice, in a punch bowl and stir well. Refrigerate until you are ready to serve.

2. Just before serving, add the ginger ale and some ice cubes, and stir.

3. Garnish the punch with the mint sprigs and lemon slices.

Servings: 40 punch cups

TAILS AND VEILS

A wedding punch guests will adore. Be sure to have plenty on hand.

1 cup sugar
Juice of 6 lemons, strained
1 cup grenadine syrup
3 46-ounce cans unsweetened pineapple juice, chilled
2 quarts ginger ale, chilled
1 quart orange sherbet, slightly softened
Garnish: Fresh strawberries and orange slices

1. Place the sugar, lemon juice, and grenadine in a large punch bowl and stir to mix well. Add the pineapple juice, stir, and refrigerate until you are ready to serve.

2. Just before serving, remove the punch from the refrigerator, add the ginger ale, and gently stir in the sherbet.

3. Place a strawberry and an orange slice in the bottom of each punch cup, and serve.

Servings: 48 punch cups

THE BRIDAL SWEET

This punch may be made in advance in large quantities.

6 cups water
10 tea bags
3 cups sugar
3 cups orange juice
3 cups unsweetened pineapple juice
1 cup strained fresh lemon juice
2 quarts ginger ale
Garnish: Mint leaves

1. Bring the water to a boil, add the tea bags, and steep for 5 minutes.

2. Remove the tea bags, add the sugar, mix, and chill for at least 3 hours.

3. Place the chilled tea in a punch bowl, add the juices, and stir.

4. Just before serving, add the ginger ale and stir. Add some ice cubes and garnish with mint leaves.

Servings: 48 punch cups

CINDERELLA'S GLASS SLIPPER

Drink a toast to your most luxurious dessert with this rosy cooler (or toast the bride and groom).

Sugar lumps (1 for each serving)
Bitters
Fresh strawberries (a few for each serving)
Lemon twists (1 for each serving)
Cold ginger ale

For each serving, put a sugar lump in the bottom of a tulip champagne glass, and add a dash of bitters, several fresh strawberries, and a lemon twist. Fill with cold ginger ale.

MILK SHRUB PUNCH

The raspberry flavor comes through to make this the award-winning punch for all time.

1 quart cold milk
1 quart raspberry sherbet
1 quart 7-Up, chilled
1 10-ounce package frozen raspberries, thawed
Garnish: Mint leaves

1. Combine the milk and sherbet in a blender in batches, blending half at a time until creamy.

2. Pour the blender mixture into a punch bowl and add some ice cubes and the soda. Stir gently.

3. Strain the raspberries and stir in the juice. Float the berries, and garnish with mint leaves.

Servings: 30 punch cups

UNREAL CHAMPAGNE

Makes a delicious toast for the bride and groom—and it's even pink!

1 cup sugar
2 cups water
2 cups unsweetened grapefruit juice
Juice of 1 lemon, strained
¼ cup grenadine syrup
2 28-ounce bottles ginger ale
Garnish: Lemon-peel strips

1. Place the sugar and the water in a small saucepan over medium heat and cook just until the sugar is dissolved, stirring constantly. Remove from the heat and allow to cool.

2. Place the grapefruit juice, lemon juice, and grenadine in a punch bowl. Add the sugar syrup and stir well. Refrigerate until you are ready to serve.

3. Just before serving, add the ginger ale and some ice cubes and stir. Ladle the punch into champagne glasses and add a strip of lemon peel to each.

Servings: 18 champagne glasses

FROSTING GLASSES

Half an hour before serving time, rinse the glasses or mugs in cold water and place them, still wet, in the freezer.

If you like, dip the rim in a saucer of sugar (for fruitades) or salt (for a vegetable drink) to coat it before freezing.

PEACHY KEEN

Toast the mother-to-be with this creamy, exciting pick-me-up. It's best with fresh peaches.

1 cup fresh, peeled, sliced peaches (or canned)
1 cup light cream
⅓ teaspoon almond extract
1 pint vanilla ice cream
2 cups cold milk
Garnish: Mint leaves

1. Combine peaches, cream, almond extract, and ice cream in a blender. Blend at high speed for 1 minute.

2. Pour into a pitcher and stir in the cold milk.

3. Serve in frosted, sugar-rimmed glasses, and top each with a mint leaf.

Servings: 4 tall glasses

FESTIVE PUNCH

Celebrate any occasion with this colorful and royally delicious punch.

3 6-ounce cans frozen lemonade concentrate
1 10-ounce package frozen strawberries, thawed
1 quart ginger ale, chilled
Ice ring
1 pint raspberry sherbet
Garnish: Whole raspberries

Prepare the lemonade according to the directions. Pour it into a punch bowl and stir in the strawberries. Just before serving, add the ginger ale and an ice ring. Then stir in the sherbet. Place a raspberry in each cup and serve the punch

Servings: 10 punch cups

FRUIT PUNCH FOR FIFTY

Nifty and thrifty for weddings, graduations, reunions and other large gatherings.

3 pounds sugar

4 quarts cold water

2 quarts finely minced pineapple, canned or fresh

1 quart unsweetened grapefruit juice

1 quart lemon juice (made from concentrate)

3 quarts orange juice

¼ cup each grated lemon and orange rind

1½ tablespoons whole cloves

10 cinnamon sticks

2 tablespoons allspice

4 cups strong, hot tea

Garnish: Wafer-thin lemon slices or frozen fruit cubes

1. Combine the sugar and water in a large soup pot. Bring to a boil, reduce the heat, and simmer for 5 minutes. Set aside to cool.

2. Strain the pineapple and place it and the fruit juices in a large punch bowl. Add the lemon and orange rind. Stir in the sugar-water mixture.

3. Put the spices in the hot tea and allow to steep for 15 minutes. Strain into the punch bowl.

4. Just before serving, add an ice block and garnish with lemon slices, or add fruit ice cubes.

Servings: 50 punch cups

MORNING MEDLEYS

A checkered tablecloth, sunshine bouncing off a bouquet of garden flowers, orange juice or canteloupe cocktails in quaint old-fashioned glasses, cinnamon buns warm from the oven . . . and over all the aroma of freshly brewed coffee beckoning your guests to celebrate a new day —this is the morning medley.

Breakfasts and brunches are wonderful occasions for entertaining. Your energy level is high, and if you use your imagination you can put together an unforgettable buffet. As a special treat surprise your own family one morning with a small bowl of punch along with the pancakes, and watch it empty before your eyes.

CANTALOUPE COCKTAIL

A country breakfast table is the perfect spot for launching these appetizing morning cocktails.

1 medium-size ripe cantaloupe, diced
3 tablespoons lime juice
2 cups orange juice
2 tablespoons sugar
¼ teaspoon vanilla extract
Pinch of salt
Garnish: Wafer-thin lime slices

1. Place all the ingredients, through the salt, in a blender and blend at low speed for 20 seconds.

2. Serve in frosted old-fashioned glasses, garnished with a lime slice.

Servings: 6 old-fashioned glasses

FRUITY FLING

Chill the juices first for the full effect.

1 quart orange juice
1 cup grapefruit juice
1 cup pineapple juice
1 pint raspberry sherbet
Garnish: Orange peel or maraschino
   cherries

Mix the juices in a large pitcher and pour over cracked ice in tall glasses. Add a scoop of raspberry sherbet, top with orange peel or a cherry, and put a straw and a long-handled spoon in each glass.

Servings: 6 tall glasses

ORANGE JUICE

Oranges are available in the supermarkets all year round and can be quite inexpensive when purchased in quantity. Sliced thin, they are always a colorful garnish for fruit-based or tea drinks. They can also be scooped clean of pulp and used as containers for fruit granites (see page 66). But we almost always think of oranges in terms of orange juice, perhaps the most popular morning juice—a delicious and refreshing way to start the day, as well as a ready source of energy.

NUMBER OF ORANGES	QUANTITY OF JUICE
1	3 oz.
4	12 oz.
8	24 oz.
20	60 oz.

A JUICE LOOSENER

To get more juice from lemons, limes, and oranges:

Squeeze the fruit when it is at room temperature. If it's still cold from the refrigerator, warm the fruit slightly in a container of hot tap water.

Or, before squeezing, roll the fruit back and forth on the counter surface, pressing hard with your palm. This softens the pulp.

DELUXE ORANGE JUICE

A velvety smooth and delicately colored juice drink. It is frothy and fancy—natural and invigorating.

1 cup (3 oranges) fresh-squeezed
    orange juice
¼ cup bottled lime juice
Powdered sugar to taste
1 unbeaten egg white
Garnish: Wafer-thin slices of orange or
    lime

1. Combine all ingredients, through the egg white, in a blender.

2. Add 3 ice cubes and blend on medium speed until well mixed and frothy.

Serves: 2 small glasses

LONG BEACH ISLAND TALL BOY

This is a terrific breakfast or brunch eye-opener.

1 6-ounce can lemonade concentrate,
    thawed
1 quart orange juice
Garnish: Strawberries and wafer-thin
    lime slices

1. Mix the lemonade in a large pitcher according to the instructions.

2. Add the orange juice and stir well.

3. Pour into frosted glasses filled with ice, and add strawberries and lime slices to each.

Servings: 8 large juice glasses

TOMATO FRAPPE

Serve these at breakfast while hungry guests are waiting for those special omelettes. Most of the preparation is done 24 hours in advance, so you can concentrate on the eggs.

1 tablespoon butter
3 tablespoons finely chopped onion
1 teaspoon sugar
1 tablespoon lemon juice
Big dash of Worcestershire sauce
4 cups tomato juice
Garnish: Lemon wedges

1. Melt the butter in a small frying pan over medium-low heat. Add the onion and sauté until golden.

2. Place the sautéed onion, sugar, lemon juice, Worcestershire sauce, and tomato juice in a blender. Blend 1 minute, or until smooth. Pour into a metal baking pan and freeze.

3. Half an hour before serving, remove the pan from the freezer. Break the tomato mixture into chunks with a fork, and blend it, on low speed a little at a time, in a blender just until smooth—don't let it melt. Serve in fancy sherbet glasses with lemon wedges and straws.

Servings: 4 to 6 sherbet glasses

MULLED TOMATO JUICE

You can make this in your electric percolator if you have a 15-cup size. It will keep the juice hot until serving time. Serve it at an elegant brunch.

2 46-ounce cans tomato juice
1 tablespoon Worcestershire sauce
1 teaspoon celery salt
½ teaspoon oregano
Dash of Tabasco sauce
½ cup butter, softened
Garnish: Sprigs of parsley or
    watercress

1. Remove the basket and holder from the percolator. Set aside. Put all the ingredients, through the butter, in the pot and perk one cycle.

2. Pour into punch cups, and serve garnished with a sprig of parsley or watercress.

Servings: 15 punch cups

CURRIED CLAM AND TOMATO

The combination of clam and curry makes this extra-special for a formal brunch. It can also be served as an appetizer at any meal.

2 cups bottled clam juice
1 cup tomato sauce *or* substitute a 16-
    ounce bottle of Clamato juice for the
    clam juice and tomato sauce
½ teaspoon curry powder

Place all the ingredients in a blender and blend for 1 minute. Pour over crushed ice in short glasses.

Servings: 6 small glasses

PINK LADY PUNCH

Great for a mid-morning brunch.

1 quart cranberry juice cocktail
1½ cups sugar
4 cups unsweetened pineapple or
    grapefruit juice
2 quarts ginger ale

1. Place the cranberry juice, sugar, and pineapple juice in a punch bowl and stir well.

2. Just before serving, add the ginger ale and ice cubes and stir.

Servings: 32 punch cups

ANNIE'S FANCY

Another exceptional punch for a bunch at brunch . . . or any time you have a large thirsty crowd.

1 cup fresh orange juice
1 cup lemonade
1 cup limeade
1 cup tangerine juice
1 46-ounce can pineapple juice
2 quarts chilled ginger ale
Garnish: Wafer-thin orange, lemon, and
    lime slices

1. Place the ingredients through the pineapple juice in a punch bowl and stir well. Refrigerate until you are ready to serve.

2. Just before serving, add the ginger ale and ice cubes and stir. Float the fruit slices on top in the punch bowl.

Servings: 40 punch cups

EVEN STEVEN

This is the traditional café au lait: easy to prepare, soothing, and especially nice served in an attractive mug or delicate teacup.

2 cups hot, fresh, strong, black coffee
2 cups hot milk (not boiling)

Carefully pour the coffee and milk *simultaneously* into your coffee cups. There should be an equal amount of each.

Servings: 4

HINTS FOR THE PERFECT CUP OF COFFEE

❖ Contrary to an old wives' tale about dirty coffee pots making the best coffee, the pot should be scrupulously clean. Coffee has a great deal of oil in it, and if it is allowed to accumulate in the pot it will add bitterness to a newly made cup.

❖ Regardless of how you brew coffee, a broken eggshell in the pot will absorb much of the bitterness and any impurities in the coffee which might make it murky.

❖ Coffee, once the can is opened or the beans are ground, loses its flavor quickly. Store it in an airtight container in the refrigerator.

❖ Be certain to use the proper grind for the method you are using:
Regular grind for percolators
Drip grind for drip pots and
vacuum coffee makers
Electroperk for electric coffee makers

❖ Measure coffee carefully. Unless you are using a coffee concentrate, measuring is the same for all methods.

❖ Regardless of which method you choose to brew coffee, after it is made it should *never* be allowed to boil. It can be kept hot in a Pyrex container inside a pan of boiling hot water.

GINGER-PEACHY COFFEE FOR A CROWD

Nothing could be better for an elegant morning brunch than this punch. The aroma alone will entice your guests!

1 cup heavy cream

2 cups cold water

3 tablespoons brown sugar

½ teaspoon ground cinnamon

¼ teaspoon ground ginger

1 10½-ounce can sliced peaches, strained (reserve the liquid)

6 cups hot, fresh, strong, black coffee

Garnish: Whipped cream and grated orange rind

1. Place the cream in a bowl and beat with a mixer until whipped. Set aside.

2. In a large saucepan over medium heat, combine the water, brown sugar, cinnamon, ginger, and reserved peach liquid. Allow the mixture to come to a boil, reduce heat and simmer for 1 minute.

3. Place the peaches and half the coffee in a blender and blend for 1 minute.

4. Add the blender mixture and the rest of the coffee to the saucepan. Stir until well mixed.

5. Serve in glass mugs, topped with a dollop of whipped cream and some grated orange rind.

Servings: 12 mugs

COFFEE MEASUREMENTS FOR ALL GRINDS

COFFEE (in tablespoons)	WATER (in cups)	SERVINGS
2	1½	2
4	3	4
6	4½	6
8	6	8
10	7½	10
½ pound	1 gallon	20
1 pound	2 gallons	40
1½ pounds	3 gallons	60

COFFEESCOTCH

Eight delicious servings of a coffee with a delicate flavor that will long be remembered by your guests. Serve cold, at a coffee klatch, especially in the warm weather.

1 cup butterscotch topping
¾ cup heavy cream
5 cups cold, strong, black coffee
1 pint coffee ice cream
Garnish: Grated nutmeg

1. Place half of each of the ingredients, through the ice cream, in a blender and blend for 30 seconds at medium speed. Pour the mixture into a pitcher and repeat with the second half of the ingredients.

2. Serve in tall glasses or coffee mugs, garnished with a grating of nutmeg.

Servings: 8 tall glasses

ORANGE COFFEE

A refreshing mid-morning drink, or wonderful at lunchtime, especially when served in a fancy goblet.

1 cup cold, strong, black coffee
1 cup cold milk
1 cup orange juice
2 tablespoons sugar
Garnish: Orange slices

Place all the ingredients, through the sugar, in a blender and blend at medium speed for 1 minute. Pour into frosted glasses and garnish each with an orange slice.

Servings: 2 large glasses

APPLE COFFEE

This is another crowd pleaser—and a perfect choice to take along on a Sunday drive in the country.

1 quart apple juice
1 quart hot, strong, black coffee
6 oranges, sliced wafer thin
2 3-inch cinnamon sticks
⅓ cup brown sugar
Pinch of ground allspice
Pinch of ground cloves

1. Place all the ingredients in a large saucepan and bring to a boil over medium heat. Reduce heat and simmer for 10 minutes.

2. Remove the saucepan from the heat and strain the liquid into a pitcher or thermos. Serve in mugs.

Servings: 8 mugs

PEANUT BUTTER COFFEE

Don't hasten to turn the page—this is worth tasting!

1 cup cold, strong, black coffee
1 cup milk
1 heaping tablespoon peanut butter
2 tablespoons sugar

Place all the ingredients in a blender and blend for 2 minutes or until smooth. Serve over ice in tall glasses.

Servings: 2 tall glasses

MOCHA COFFEE

Serve this either hot or cold, depending on the weather. It is excellent following a meal, or in the morning instead of regular coffee.

1 tablespoon powdered instant coffee
1 teaspoon chocolate syrup
1 cup milk, heated to the boiling point *or* 1 cup boiling water with 1 tablespoon heavy cream *or* 1 cup cold milk

Hot: Mix together the instant coffee and syrup in a coffee cup. Add the hot milk, or boiling water and cream, stir, and serve.

Cold: Place the instant coffee, syrup, and cold milk in a blender and blend until well mixed. Pour into a tall glass over ice. (Instead of 1 cup milk, try half milk and half cream, or half milk and half club soda.)

Servings: 1 cup

MOCHA

Combine equal quantities of hot chocolate and strong coffee. Pour into cups and top with whipped cream—then sprinkle with grated nutmeg or orange peel.

EASY ESPRESSO

For each serving use 3 ounces of fresh cold water to each coffee measure of Italian roast drip grind coffee. Prepare in regular drip pot and serve in demitasse cups or in wine glasses with a twist of lemon peel, and some sugar cubes for dunking.

INSTANT COFFEE FOR A CROWD

For the mid-morning coffee break at, let's say, the dress rehearsal of your club's annual play, invite the entire cast and crew to this quick pick-me-up.

1 cup instant coffee
6 quarts cold water

Combine instant coffee and water in a large pot. Heat just to boiling and ladle out immediately.

Servings: 32 coffee cups

ASIAN ICED COFFEE

Cardamom gives this drink its unusual flavor. Serve it with some exotic pastries.

4 cups cold water
1 teaspoon cardamom seeds
8 tablespoons ground coffee
Sugar to taste
Garnish: Pineapple cubes

1. Place the water and cardamom seeds in a medium saucepan and bring to a boil over high heat. Continue boiling, uncovered, for 3 minutes.

2. Set up a drip coffee pot with the measured amount of ground coffee.

3. Pour the cardamom water over the coffee grounds, sweeten the coffee to taste, and allow to cool.

4. Strain over ice in tall glasses, garnished with a pineapple cube.

Servings: 4 tall glasses

ICED COFFEE PARK AVENUE

An exotic taste you will enjoy over and over again.

2 cups hot, strong, black coffee
½ teaspoon bitters
½ teaspoon vanilla extract
1 tablespoon sugar
12 coffee ice cubes (see page 8)
1 quart club soda
Garnish: Wafer-thin orange slices and
  maraschino cherries

1. Place all the ingredients, through the sugar, in a large heat-resistant pitcher. Stir well and allow to cool.

2. Place 2 coffee ice cubes in each of 6 glasses. Divide the coffee mixture equally among the glasses.

3. Fill the glasses to the top with club soda, and garnish with an orange slice and cherry toothpick.

Servings: 6 tall glasses

THE CZAR'S TODDY

This is a recipe for a dry mix that can be stored in a covered container. It is excellent to keep on hand any time of the year as an instant beverage at home or in your desk drawer.

3 cups sugar

2 cups orange-flavored breakfast drink (powdered concentrate)

1 cup unsweetened instant tea mix

1 teaspoon ground cloves

1 teaspoon ground cinnamon

1. In a medium-size bowl, combine all the ingredients and mix well. Store in an airtight container.

2. To serve, put 2 rounded tablespoons of mix in each cup. Fill with boiling water and stir well.

Servings: 32 teacups

TEA

The proverbial teapot is a warm way to welcome one guest or many. There are literally hundreds of kinds of tea, and it's fun to have a variety on hand, in loose form or in tea bags. Since the flavors vary quite a bit—from the delicate Oolong to the smoky Souchong or the many spicy blends which are available—you should experiment to see which appeals to you the most.

Teapot tea is best when preparing more than one cup at a time. It is always good to preheat the pot: rinse it with boiling water. Then, measure the loose tea into the pot—½ to 1 teaspoon of tea per cup of water, according to the strength you like. Pour in the boiling water. You will see the tea leaves begin to float. Put the cover on the pot and allow it to stand for 3 to 5 minutes—any longer and the tea will acquire a bitter taste. Then pour the tea through a tea strainer into each cup. (Antique silver tea strainers with ornate handles are a lovely addition to a formal tea.)

You can eliminate messy straining by purchasing a tea ball—a small strainer with a screw-on lid that is filled with loose tea and placed directly in the teapot before adding the boiling water.

Whether making cold or hot tea, you should always use a glass, china, or earthenware pot or pitcher. Metal changes the flavor of tea.

CHOCOLATE SIN

Warm and wonderful—goes well with an intense game of backgammon.

1   ounce unsweetened chocolate
¼ cup sugar
Dash of vanilla
Dash of ground cinnamon
Pinch of salt
3 cups milk
Garnish: Whipped cream or mini
    marshmallows

1. Carefully melt the chocolate over very low heat, or in the top of a double boiler over simmering water.

2. Add the spices and the milk and stir to mix well. Heat until very hot but not boiling. Serve with a dollop of whipped cream or float some marshmallows on top.

Servings: 2 mugs

CHOCOLATE WHIPPED CREAM

Regular hot coffee—prepared by any method—becomes doubly delicious when topped with chocolate whipped cream.

1 pint heavy cream
3 heaping tablespoons cocoa mix
3 heaping tablespoons sugar
½ teaspoon vanilla extract

Combine all the ingredients in a bowl and whip with a mixer until the cream forms peaks.

DECORATING WITH CHOCOLATE

To grate chocolate: Chill a square of baking chocolate first, then put it through a hand grinder. You can use a cheese grater but be sure to go slowly to prevent knuckle scrapes.

For decorative curls: Bring the chocolate to room temperature. Shave off thin strips with a sharp paring knife or a vegetable peeler.

COCOA HONEY

For lazing around with the Sunday papers or at bedtime with a good novel.

1 quart milk
1 cinnamon stick
¼ cup powdered cocoa
Pinch of salt
¼ cup honey

1. Place the milk with the cinnamon stick in a medium saucepan and scald over low heat. Remove from the heat.

2. Remove the cinnamon stick and discard. Pour ½ cup of the hot milk into a small bowl and stir in the cocoa and salt.

3. Return the cocoa mixture to the remaining hot milk, place over low heat, and gradually stir in the honey. Serve in warmed mugs.

Servings: 4 mugs

BORED-WITH-COCOA COCOA

Mmmm! Keep some anise flavoring on hand so you can offer this unusual drink to a special guest on a moment's notice.

3 tablespoons chocolate syrup
1 cup hot milk
1 teaspoon anise

Combine the syrup and milk in a cup and stir in the anise.

Servings: 1

COCOA SUPREME

Ordinary cocoa becomes richer with a little half and half.

4 heaping teaspoons powdered cocoa
Dash of salt
4 teaspoons sugar
1 cup boiling water
3 cups half and half, heated
Garnish: Marshmallows

1. Combine cocoa, salt, and sugar in a small bowl.

2. Put 1 teaspoon of the mixture in each mug, then add ¼ cup water and fill with half and half. Stir well and float a marshmallow on top.

CHOCOLATE DELUXE

For those with discerning taste. Don't forget to pass the butter cookies.

4 egg whites
¾ cup powdered cocoa
Pinch of ground cinnamon
½ cup sugar
2 quarts milk
Garnish: Whipped cream or chocolate
  shavings

1. Combine the egg whites, cocoa, cinnamon, sugar, and ½ cup of the milk in a blender. Blend for 15 seconds at medium speed.

2. Pour blender mixture into a large saucepan, and add the rest of the milk. Heat until very hot but not boiling. Pour into pretty teacups and garnish each with whipped cream or chocolate shavings.

Servings: 8 teacups

BASHES, BBQS, BEACH PARTIES

Summer's arrived and so has a thirst for long, cool drinks. You'll want to be prepared when friends drop by for an informal backyard barbecue, the kids come home from a successful little league game, or when a neighbor needs a tasty reward after mowing the lawn. Take advantage of all those fabulous summer fruits and vegetables—and remember, there's a whole world beyond plain old iced tea!

If the great weather signals a beach day, many of these recipes can be poured into a thermos and carried off to enjoy after a swim.

HALFSHELLS

A zesty appetizer to serve to tired sailors, or before the main meal at a clambake.

¼ cup chopped celery
1 small onion, finely chopped
1 teaspoon horseradish
¼ cup ketchup or chili sauce
2 cups bottled clam juice
Garnish: Wafer-thin lemon slices

1. Place all the ingredients through the ketchup in a blender and liquefy.

2. Turn the blender off and slowly add the clam juice. Stir gently.

3. Serve over ice with a slice of lemon in each glass.

BASIC ICED TEA

This is a quick method for making a delicious iced tea. If you have some on hand, use fresh pineapple cut into spears as stirrers.

2 ounces (about ⅔ cup) loose tea,
   or 6 tea bags
1 quart boiling water
3 quarts cold tap water
Sugar to taste (optional)
Garnish: Lemon slices

1. Place the tea in a teapot and add the boiling water. Stir, and allow to steep for 6 minutes.

2. Place the cold water in a punch bowl with ice. Strain the concentrated tea into the cold water and stir. Add sugar to taste.

3. Serve with lemon slices and place a stirrer in each glass.

Servings: 20

SOLAR SENSATION

Here's a way to make iced tea in the backyard on one of those hot summer days when you can't bear to heat up the kitchen and you're in no particular rush.

3 quarts cold water
8 tea bags
Sugar and lemon to taste
Garnish: Mint sprigs

1. Place the cold water and tea bags in a large pot and set it in a spot that will remain sunny most of the day.

2. At dinner time, remove the tea bags and add the sugar and lemon to taste (or allow guests to add their own). Serve over ice with a mint sprig in each glass.

Servings: 12

SPECIAL 'N QUICK ICED TEA

This is a tangy, carbonated version of the classic iced tea.

6 tea bags
3 cups boiling water
1 28-ounce bottle 7-Up
Garnish: Wafer-thin lemon, lime, or
    orange slices

1. Place the tea bags in a teapot and add the boiling water. Stir, and allow to steep for 3 to 5 minutes.

2. Pour the tea into a large pitcher and chill. When ready to serve, stir in the 7-Up.

3. Serve over ice cubes in tall glasses garnished with a fruit slice.

Servings: 6 tall glasses

LIME 'N LEMONADE

A wonderful way to welcome summer guests of all ages to a garden banquet.

5 cups water
1½ cups sugar
½ cup fresh lemon juice
1 6-ounce can limeade concentrate
2 12-ounce bottles ginger ale
Garnish: Mint sprigs

1. Combine water and sugar in a medium saucepan and place over medium heat. Cook, stirring, until sugar is dissolved. Put aside to cool.

2. Stir the lemon juice and limeade concentrate into the sugar syrup, mixing thoroughly. Pour into a large pitcher or a punch bowl.

3. Just before serving, add some ice and stir in the ginger ale. Add mint sprigs as garnish.

Servings: 16 punch cups

HAWAIIAN HULA SHAKE

Great for a summer luau.

1 cup fresh coconut milk (see page 18)
1 cup pineapple juice
1 teaspoon coconut extract
½ cup chocolate syrup
1 cup vanilla ice cream
Garnish: Maraschino cherries and
   pineapple cubes skewered on
   toothpicks

1. Put all the ingredients, through the ice cream, in a blender and blend on medium speed for 15 seconds or until smooth.

2. Pour into tall frosted glasses. Add cherry-and-pineapple garnish to each.

Servings: 4 tall glasses

TROPICAL CUCUMBER

Perfect for taking to the beach in a cooler. This recipe makes a large quantity—it'll keep nicely in the refrigerator.

2 cups sugar
2 quarts cold water
Peel of 2 lemons
1½ cups fresh lemon juice (8 lemons)
1 cup fresh lime juice (6 limes)
1 cup thinly sliced cucumber
Lemonade ice cubes (see page 8)
Garnish: Mint leaves

1. Combine the sugar and 2 cups of the water in a large saucepan. Boil for 1 minute. Remove from heat.

2. Add the lemon peel to the sugar syrup and allow to steep for 7 minutes. Remove the peel.

3. Add the remaining water, the lemon and lime juices, and the cucumber to the sugar syrup. Stir well and chill.

4. Just before leaving for the beach, put some lemonade ice cubes in a cooler and add the punch. Take along some mint leaves for garnish, if you like.

Servings: 12 plastic tumblers

SUGAR SYRUP

Ready-made sweetener for fresh fruit drinks.

3 cups water
3 cups granulated sugar

Boil sugar and water together in a medium saucepan for 5 minutes. Store in a covered container after cooling.

MOLLY PITCHER

Ever wonder how to glorify barbecued hot dogs? This is it! You can make this a July 4th Special by serving it over ice cube flags. See the instructions for ice cubes, page 8.

2 cups cranberry juice cocktail
2 cups pineapple juice
¼ teaspoon almond extract
1 quart 7-Up

1. Combine the juices and the almond extract in a large pitcher. Mix well and refrigerate.

2. Just before serving, add the 7-Up, stir, and pour over ice in tall glasses.

Servings: 4 tall glasses

SUMMER DELIGHT

Orange and chocolate together is a delicious combination.

2 cups orange juice
1 pint chocolate ice cream
1 quart ginger ale
Garnish: Grated orange peel and
    maraschino cherries

1. Place the orange juice and ice cream in a blender. Blend at medium speed for 30 seconds or until smooth.

2. Fill glasses three-quarters full with crushed ice. Fill each glass halfway with ginger ale, then add the blender mixture, stirring gently.

3. Garnish with grated orange peel and a maraschino cherry.

Servings: 8 tall glasses

CABAÑA DELIGHT

Scoop this out at the beach or at the poolside for thirsty swimmers and sun worshipers.

2 cups orange juice
2 cups cold milk
2 eggs
½ cup honey
1 banana, cut in pieces
1 pint vanilla ice cream
Garnish: Maraschino cherries

1. Place all the ingredients through the banana into a blender and blend until smooth.

2. Pour into tall glasses over cracked ice, add a scoop of ice cream, and top with a cherry.

Servings: 6 tall glasses

THE PINK SNOWMAN

This is so beautiful and delicious. Serve it in delicate goblets or tall soda glasses.

1 cup orange juice
1 10-ounce package frozen
   strawberries, partially thawed
½ cup water
2 large scoops vanilla ice cream
Garnish: Strawberries or orange slices

1. Combine the juice, berries, and water in a blender. Blend at medium speed for 30 seconds.

2. Pour into tall glasses or goblets and add a scoop of ice cream to each. Garnish with fruit, add a straw, and serve immediately.

Servings: 2 large goblets or glasses

ORANGE SWIZZLE

Tart and tangy . . .

1 6½-ounce can frozen orange juice,
   thawed
1 quart ginger ale
Garnish: Orange slices and maraschino
   cherries

1. Fill 4 tall glasses with ice cubes.

2. Place a heaping tablespoon of orange juice concentrate in each glass, and fill with ginger ale. Stir to blend thoroughly.

3. Top with orange slices and cherries, add a decorative straw, and serve.

Servings: 4 tall glasses

ORANGE GRANITE

12 oranges, approximately
2 cups sugar
1 quart water
Garnish: Maraschino cherries, orange
  slices, or lemon slices

1. Peel 6 oranges cleanly. Slice the peeled oranges, remove any seeds, and place the slices in a wide bowl. Sprinkle with the sugar. Set aside for several hours to make a syrup.

2. Once the syrup has formed, squeeze the juice from the other 6 oranges or as many as it takes to yield about 3 cups and add it to the syrup.

3. Add the water, mix well, and strain into a freezer container. Freeze until a light frosting appears.

4. Serve in small glasses garnished with fruit.

Servings: 8 to 10 small glasses

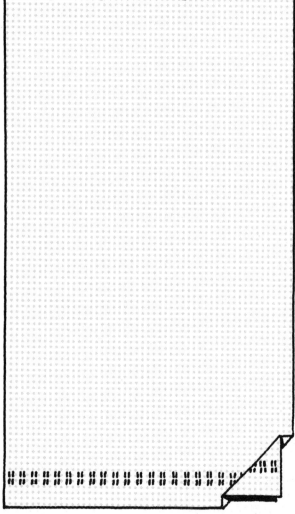

FRUIT GRANITES

Summer fruits make refreshing "granites," a favorite drink in France that was adopted from the Italian "granitii." The granite resembles snow-frosted water. It must always be liquid enough to be poured into a glass.

BERRY GRANITE

1 quart fresh strawberries, hulled and washed *or* 1 quart fresh raspberries, washed
3 cups sugar
1 tablespoon strawberry (raspberry) extract
2 cups water
Garnish: Sliced strawberries

1. Place the berries in a shallow bowl and cover with the sugar. Set aside to form a syrup.

2. Once the syrup has formed, place a sieve over a medium-size bowl, and pour the syrup through, pressing with a wooden spoon to extract all the juice.

3. Add the extract and the water and mix well. Pour into a freezer container and freeze until a light frosting appears.

4. Serve in small glasses garnished with strawberry slices or whole raspberries.

Servings: 4 small glasses

MY THREE SUNS

A bright refresher. Quick, elegant, and scrumptious!

2 cups orange juice
1 quart apple juice
1 pint strawberry sherbet
Garnish: Orange peel

1. Pour orange juice and apple juice into a large pitcher and stir well.

2. Fill tall frosted glasses with cracked ice and add the juice.

3. Top each glass with a scoop of sherbet, garnish with orange peel, and add a straw.

Servings: 8 tall glasses

TALL PAUL

A backyard, over-the-fence cooler offer.

2 cups cold orange juice
1 banana, cut in pieces
1 cup heavy cream
Garnish: Orange slices

Combine all the ingredients in a blender and blend for 15 seconds at high speed. Pour into tall glasses and top each with an orange slice.

Servings: 2 tall glasses

MELONADE

A beautiful addition to any summer party, served in a melon bowl.

1 medium-size ripe watermelon (6 cups juice)
1 cup lemon juice
2 cups orange juice
2 cups sugar dissolved in 2 cups hot water *or* 2 cups prepared sugar syrup (see page 62)
2 28-ounce bottles 7-Up
Dash of grenadine (optional)
Garnish: Sliced limes, whole small strawberries, or a combination of sliced oranges and bananas

1. Cut the watermelon in half by scalloping. Remove the seeds, and put the pulp into a blender and purée (in batches). This should yield about 6 cups of juice.

2. Combine the watermelon juice, the lemon and orange juices, and the sugar syrup in a large pitcher. Stir well.

3. When ready to serve, place some ice cubes in the melon bowl and add the juice mixture. Carefully mix in the 7-Up. You may want to add some grenadine for color.

4. Garnish the punch with fruit, and ladle into punch cups.

Servings: 30 punch cups

WATERMELON PUNCH BOWL

This makes a decorative container for any kind of party punch—especially pretty if you use pink or green or clear glass punch cups.

Using a sharp knife, cut 1½-inch zigzags around the center of the melon from end to end. Be sure to cut as deep into the melon as you can. Pull the melon apart and scoop out the pulp with a large spoon.

You can use both parts if you cut the melon perfectly in half. Or for one large bowl, make the cut closer to the top so you have a deeper bowl.

FAST FRUIT PUNCH

This punch can be carried in a cooler to beaches, streams, fields, games, and gatherings of every kind. You may lose the fizz from the ginger ale, but not the flavor.

1 quart ginger ale

1 46-ounce can pineapple juice

1 32-ounce bottle grape juice

1 6-ounce can frozen orange juice, prepared according to instructions on can

1 6-ounce can frozen lemonade, prepared according to instructions on can

Garnish: Fresh fruit of any kind

Combine all the ingredients, through the lemonade, in a large punch bowl and stir gently. Add ice and fruit garnish.

If you're taking it in a cooler, make sure all the ingredients are well chilled first. You can make lemonade ice cubes (see page 8) instead of stirring in the lemonade—that way the flavor won't be diluted in the summer sun!

Servings: 40 (about 5½ quarts)

NECTAR OF NECTARINES

Fresh and fruity, cool and fast. Try this also with peaches, blueberries, blackberries, strawberries, or raspberries. It can be stored in the refrigerator or taken along in a small thermos.

3 or 4 nectarines, peeled and sliced, to make 1 cup slices
½ cup fresh orange juice
1 tablespoon lemon juice
1 tablespoon sugar
1 cup finely cracked ice

Place all the ingredients in a blender and blend for about 1 minute at medium speed, until smooth.

Servings: 1 tall glass

WAGON WHEELS

Simple enough to make, but unusual because of the garnish.

½ cup cold orange juice
½ cup cold apple cider
Garnish: Anchor a maraschino cherry to both sides of a thick orange slice with a toothpick

Fill a tall glass with ice, add the juices, and stir. Top with a "wagon wheel." Insert a straw if you like.

Servings: 1

RHUBARB PUNCH

This is a bit time-consuming to make, but your efforts will be rewarded by lavish praise from your guests.

1½ pounds rhubarb, cut into small
   pieces
1 quart water
1½ cups sugar
½ cup orange juice
Juice of 1 lemon
Pinch of salt
1 quart ginger ale
Garnish: Fresh mint leaves

1. Place rhubarb and water in a large saucepan, bring to a boil, and cook over low heat until the fruit is soft. Strain into a saucepan. You may reserve the pulp for another use. Add 1½ cups of sugar to the strained juice and heat to boiling, stirring to mix well. Set aside to cool.

2. Add the orange juice, lemon juice, and salt. Refrigerate until ready to serve.

3. Just before serving, place some ice in a punch bowl, pour in the punch, and add the ginger ale. Top with mint leaves.

Servings: 12 punch cups

HANDYMAN'S PUNCH

A tea-based punch — good for a September beach crowd, when fresh apple cider is on hand.

2 cups extra-strong tea, chilled
1 quart apple cider
¼ cup fresh lemon juice
1 quart cold ginger ale
Garnish: Wafer-thin lemon slices

1. Combine tea, cider, and lemon juice in a punch bowl and stir.

2. Just before serving, add some ice cubes and stir in the ginger ale. Top with lemon slices.

Servings: 24 punch cups

CREOLE LEMONADE

An old Creole recipe, this makes a glorious summer punch.

2 cups sugar
3 quarts water
12 lemons, juiced
1 pineapple, freshly sliced and juiced in a blender
2 quarts seltzer or club soda
12 lemons, sliced very thin
36 thin slices pineapple
Fresh, ripe strawberries

1. Place sugar, water, lemon juice, and pineapple juice into a large punch bowl. Mix well.

2. When you are ready to serve, place a large block of ice in the punch bowl and stir in the seltzer. Add the fruit.

3. Place some crushed ice in each punch cup, and then fill with lemonade.

Servings: 36 punch cups

CHERRY JUBILEE

You might try this one as a liquid dessert following a summer dinner.

2 cups strong coffee, chilled
½ pint cherry ice cream
1 tablespoon maraschino cherry juice
Garnish: Maraschino cherries

1. Place the coffee, ice cream, and cherry juice in a blender and blend at medium speed for 30 seconds, or until smooth.

2. Pour into chilled punch cups and top each with a cherry.

Servings: 4 punch cups

JIMMY'S CLASSIC LIMEADE

Frost some tall, thin glasses for this standby thirst quencher.

4 tablespoons fresh lime juice
2 tablespoons sugar *or* ¼ cup sugar
    syrup (see page 62)
1 cup cold water
Garnish: Mint sprig

Combine all the ingredients in a small bowl or pitcher. Stir well and serve over ice cubes in a tall glass with a sprig of mint.

Servings: 1

GARNISHES

FOR FRUIT AND MILK DRINKS

Mint leaves
Lemon or lime slices
Orange slices
Cantaloupe, thinly sliced
Red and green
   maraschino cherries
Whipped cream
Chocolate whipped
   cream
Candy canes
Peppermint candies
Jelly beans
Cinnamon sticks
Pineapple chunks
   (skewered on
   toothpicks with
   cherries)
Fresh strawberries
Cranberries
Raspberries
Shaved chocolate
Nutmeg
Shredded coconut
Grapes
Melon balls
Raisins

FOR VEGETABLE DRINKS

Parsley
Watercress
Celery sticks
Cucumber sticks
Carrot sticks
Carrot curls
Cherry tomatoes
Scallions
Chopped chives
Paprika
Freshly ground
   pepper
Black or green
   olives
Cocktail onions

EASY MEXICAN COFFEE

This is good for any kind of a crowd, any time of the year—but it sure livens up a Fourth of July celebration.

1 vanilla bean
3 large cinnamon sticks
¾ cup espresso or dark-roasted coffee grounds
10 cups cold water
½ cup heavy cream
Dark brown sugar to taste

1. Place vanilla bean and cinnamon sticks in the bottom of the coffee pot and brew the coffee (any machine method), using the 10 cups of water. Discard the grounds. Keep the coffee hot.

2. Whip the cream, adding brown sugar to taste, until stiff.

3. Pour the hot coffee into cups, and top each with some whipped cream.

Servings: 16 coffee cups

LEMON COFFEE

This recipe is for two tall servings and is perfect late in the afternoon. By increasing the quantities, this can be a very good punch for any occasion.

2 cups cold, strong, black coffee
1 cup lemon sherbet, slightly softened
1 tablespoon grated lemon rind
1 tablespoon lemon juice
2 tablespoons sugar
Garnish: Maraschino cherries

Place all the ingredients, through the sugar, in a blender and blend at medium speed for 2 minutes. Serve in frosted glasses, garnished with a cherry.

Servings: 2 tall glasses

AUDREY'S SPICED AND ICED COFFEE

Audrey's recipes are the best! Try this winsome blend of spices and coffee.

1 3-inch cinnamon stick
4 whole cloves
6 tablespoons sugar
4 cups strong hot coffee
Garnish: Vanilla ice cream or heavy cream

1. Add the spices and sugar to a pot of freshly brewed coffee. Stir and let it cool to room temperature, then pour into a glass pitcher and chill in the refrigerator.

2. Remove the cloves and cinnamon stick, and serve over ice in tall glasses with a bit of ice cream or heavy cream stirred in.

Servings: 4 tall glasses

RUTH'S RICO CHICO

A savory Mexican coffee—just perfect for topping off an intimate outdoor dinner.

2 tablespoons chocolate syrup
½ cup heavy cream
¼ teaspoon ground cinnamon
2 tablespoons sugar
Pinch of nutmeg
2 cups strong hot coffee
Garnish: Whipped cream and ground cinnamon

1. Place the chocolate syrup, heavy cream, cinnamon, sugar, and nutmeg into a small bowl, stir, then whip.

2. Pour the hot coffee into 4 mugs and add the syrup mixture, stirring gently. Top with whipped cream, and sprinkle with extra cinnamon.

Serves: 4 mugs

CAMPFIRE COFFEE

For hunting and fishing trips, wilderness adventures and any other adventures around the campfire.

5 quarts plus 1 cup cold water
1½ cups regular-grind coffee
1 egg

1. In a large pot placed over a charcoal fire or campfire, bring the 5 quarts of water to a rolling boil.

2. Place the coffee, egg, and ½ cup of cold water in a bowl and mix well. Pour this coffee mixture into the boiling water and return it to a boil.

3. Immediately remove the coffee from the heat and add the last ½ cup of cold water. The coffee grounds will sink to the bottom of the pot.

4. Ladle the coffee into tin mugs or paper cups.

Servings: 30

SCHOOL DAYS, SCHOOL DAYS

Good old golden rule days. This is the time of year when you move indoors and extend an autumn welcome to your friends. If you have tended a garden, chances are you have a bushel or two of tomatoes just waiting to be cooked up in an exciting spicy drink. And with the harvest just beginning in the apple orchards and cranberry bogs, fresh cider and cranberries are everywhere, and fall is in the air.

School box lunches need a thermos with a treat. Halloween is on the horizon—tiny thirsty witches and goblins appear on your threshold. Thanksgiving festivities spark your flair for entertaining—try Cucumber Punch as an appetizer, or a giant bowl of Pilgrim's Cider, or the Family Thanksgiving Punch, the ultimate in color and flavor.

HOME MADE SPICY TOMATO JUICE

Refer to your favorite canning instructions for this one—a great way to use up the not-so-perfect tomatoes in your own garden, or to take advantage of bushel bargains at a farm market. You'll have enough juice to get you through all the bleak days of winter. (If you don't have the equipment for canning, cut the quantities down and make just enough for a great Thanksgiving dinner appetizer —and maybe extra for a day or two after.)

½ bushel ripe tomatoes, quartered
6 large carrots, peeled and cut in pieces
2 large green peppers, seeded and cut in pieces
4 medium onions, peeled and chopped
Half a bunch of celery, cleaned and cut in pieces
1 bunch parsley, washed
Worcestershire sauce to taste
Garlic powder to taste
Salt and pepper to taste
Lemon juice, sugar, or onion juice for extra flavor

1. Place all the ingredients through the parsley in a large soup pot, bring to a boil, reduce heat, and simmer until soft.

2. Place a colander in a large bowl, and strain the juice through it, pressing down hard to extract all the liquid.

3. Flavor to taste with the seasonings and can in airtight jars following your usual canning instructions.

4. Serve over crushed ice with an additional seasoning of lemon or onion juice, or some sugar.

Servings: 12 quarts

CUPBOARD KEEPER: TOMATO JUICE À LA BLENDER

Blend any of the following combinations into a cup of tomato or tomato-vegetable juice for a low-calorie taste treat.

❖ ¼ cup chopped cucumber
   Salt and pepper to taste

❖ ½ cup chopped green pepper
   Dash of onion juice
   Dash of Tabasco sauce
   Salt and pepper to taste

❖ 2 fresh basil leaves
      (or ½ teaspoon dried basil)
   1 teaspoon chopped onion
   Dash of Tabasco sauce
   Salt and pepper to taste

❖ 1 clove garlic, chopped
   Dash of lemon juice
   Salt and pepper to taste

❖ 3 tablespoons lime juice
   Dash of Tabasco sauce

❖ ½ cup clam juice
   1 tablespoon lime juice
   Dash of Worcestershire sauce

❖ ½ cup plain yogurt
   1 tablespoon chopped onion
   Salt and pepper to taste

SUNSET SAUCE

A hearty tomato drink.

10 ounces stewed tomatoes, fresh or
   canned
2 tablespoons lemon juice
2 tablespoons lime juice
1 cup cold water
Garnish: Wafer-thin lime slices

1. Place the stewed tomatoes and the juices in a blender and blend for 30 seconds on medium speed.

2. Add the cold water, stir, and pour into old-fashioned glasses filled with crushed ice. Garnish each with a slice of lime.

Servings: 6 old-fashioned glasses

THE BUFFALO CHILL

Wildly spicy and delectable. Serve at a fall picnic (bring it along in a thermos) or at a backyard gathering.

1 46-ounce can tomato juice
1 cucumber, peeled and grated
3 scallions, finely chopped
4 tablespoons lemon juice
2 tablespoons Worcestershire sauce
Dash of Tabasco sauce
Pinch of garlic salt
Salt and pepper to taste
Garnish: Parsley sprigs

1. Place all the ingredients, through the salt and pepper, in a large pitcher and stir. Refrigerate for 1 hour.

2. Before serving, strain the juice, then pour into old-fashioned glasses and garnish each with a parsley sprig.

Servings: 8 old-fashioned glasses

TOMATO HURRY-CURRY

Bring a big thermos of this to the beach along with a bag of peanuts for an energizing end-of-the-season treat.

1 46-ounce can tomato juice
1 teaspoon curry powder
Dash of Tabasco

1. Place ½ cup of the tomato juice in a small bowl, add the curry powder, and stir well to blend. Put this mixture into a large saucepan and add the remaining tomato juice and the Tabasco. Heat just to boiling. Refrigerate.

2. Pour chilled juice into a thermos just before you leave for the beach.

Servings: 6 paper cups or mugs

CUCUMBER PUNCH

Cucumbers are abundant at the end of summer and can be prepared a number of ways for tasty drinks. This one is a good, hearty punch, perfect for a fall luncheon.

1 10 ½-ounce can condensed tomato
  soup
2 cups buttermilk
½ teaspoon curry powder
½ teaspoon Worcestershire sauce
3 cucumbers, peeled and finely diced
Garnish: Cucumber slices and freshly
  ground pepper

1. Place soup, buttermilk, and spices in a blender and blend for 30 seconds at low speed. Add diced cucumber and stir.

2. Pour into glass mugs and top with cucumber slices and a sprinkling of black pepper.

Servings: 6 mugs

CELERY, ANYONE?

For a tasty, nourishing vegetable highball, combine celery and tomato juices.

2 cups tomato or tomato-vegetable
  juice
1 cup celery juice
Garnish: Stuffed green olives

Combine the juices in a pitcher and stir well. Serve in tall glasses with an olive or two in each.

Servings: 2 tall glasses

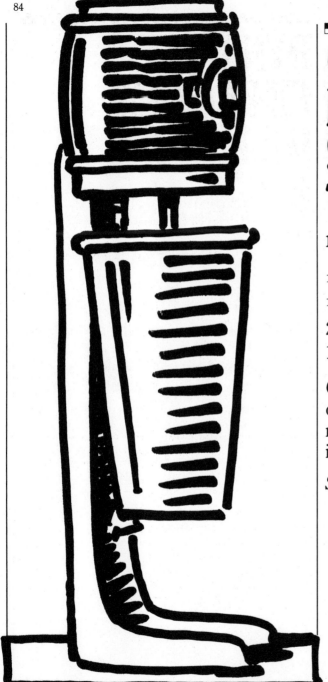

CHOCOLATE MALTED MILK SHAKE

The kind your grandfather remembers.

¼ cup malt powder
½ cup chocolate syrup
2 large scoops chocolate ice cream
1½ cups cold milk

Combine all the ingredients in a blender or milk-shake machine. Blend at medium speed for 2 minutes and pour into a tall glass.

Servings: 2

CUPBOARD KEEPERS: CHOCOLATE PLUS

For great flavor, add any one of the following to a cup of hot cocoa or cold chocolate milk:

❖ Wedge of lemon, lime, or orange (squeezed into cocoa made with water only)

❖ Dash of vanilla, almond, or rum extract

❖ 1 teaspoon cherry, raspberry, or strawberry syrup

❖ 1 heaping tablespoon vanilla ice cream

❖ Use a candy cane for a stirrer

❖ Float mini-marshmallows

❖ Top with grated chocolate or coconut

DYNAMITE CHOCOLATE DRAGONS

At teenage parties or sleepovers during the holidays, make any number of these.

⅓ cup chocolate syrup
1½ cups cold milk
2 teaspoons sugar
1 cup vanilla ice cream
Garnish: Grated chocolate

Place all the ingredients in a blender and blend until smooth. Pour into tall glasses and top with the grated chocolate.

Servings: 2 tall glasses

PEANUT BUTTER 'N JELLY

This is a drinkable sandwich. Children love it!

4 cups cold milk
1 cup peanut butter
1 teaspoon vanilla extract
2 tablespoons currant jelly
1 pint chocolate ice cream

1. Place half of each of the ingredients in a blender and blend until smooth. Pour the mixture into a pitcher and repeat with the other half.

2. Serve in tall glasses, each with a different colored straw.

Servings: 6 tall glasses

GRAPE SHAKE

This is a very sweet milk shake, and because of its pretty lavender color it looks divine. Even if you make it for yourself, make it special by frosting your mug.

1 cup milk
½ cup grape juice
Large scoop vanilla ice cream

Combine milk, grape juice, and ice cream in a blender and blend for 1 minute at medium speed. Pour into a frosted glass or mug.

Servings: 1

CRANBERRY CREAM SHAKE

A milk shake with a cranberry-orange flavor. Beware, this could be habit-forming—especially for those with a taste for the tart!

1 4-ounce can whole cranberry sauce
1 quart orange juice
1 pint vanilla ice cream
Garnish: Slice of orange

1. Combine the cranberry sauce, juice, and ice cream in a blender. Do this in batches, half each time. Blend for 30 seconds.

2. Pour into tall glasses with a slice of orange perched on the rim.

Servings: 6 tall glasses

BANANA MILK SHAKE

Goes down the hatch really smoothly.

2 cups milk
2 bananas, cut in pieces
1 pint vanilla ice cream, softened
Garnish: Grated nutmeg

Put milk, bananas, and ice cream into a blender or a milk-shake machine. Mix at high speed until smooth. Pour into tall glasses and sprinkle with nutmeg.

Servings: 6 tall glasses

BANANA COFFEE SHAKE

For the adult crowd, give this a whirl in your blender, and chances are you will make it again and again.

2 or 3 bananas, cut in pieces
2 cups cold coffee
1 pint vanilla ice cream
1 teaspoon vanilla extract
⅓ cup sugar
Garnish: Maraschino cherries

Put all the ingredients, through the sugar, in a blender. Blend for 1 minute at medium speed. Serve in frosted mugs or glasses, topped with a cherry.

Servings: 4 mugs

BARRISTER'S DESSERT SHAKE

This delicate combination of coffee and banana—sweet and creamy—is actually dessert and coffee all in one!

½ cup light cream
2 cups strong coffee, chilled
4 teaspoons sugar
2 bananas, sliced
Garnish: Shredded coconut

Combine all the ingredients through the banana in a blender and blend at high speed until smooth. Serve topped with a bit of shredded coconut.

Servings: 4 glasses

MONKEY SEE, MONKEY DO

Buy a can of coconut cream at the grocery store and try this out on the kids when they're busy playing games. You will soon be making seconds.

⅓ cup coconut cream
½ cup lemon sherbet, softened
2 cups 7-Up, chilled
Garnish: Wafer-thin lime slices

1. Divide the coconut cream and lemon sherbet between 2 tall glasses, and stir well.

2. Add a few ice cubes, and fill the glasses with the 7-Up. Stir gently, and top each with a slice of lime.

Servings: 2 tall glasses

BABY ROY'S CHOCOLATE PEPPERMINT

A refreshing, cold drink. Children love this one, especially when it's served with a peppermint candy stirrer.

1 4½-ounce can chocolate syrup
1 quart cold milk
1 teaspoon peppermint extract
1 pint chocolate ice cream
Garnish: Whipped cream, peppermint
  sticks for stirrers

Place all the ingredients, through the ice cream, in a blender and blend for 1 minute or until smooth. Pour into tall glasses, top with whipped cream, and add a candy stirrer.

Servings: 6 tall glasses

GINGER ALE FLOAT

Floats and sodas are thirst-quenching, and can be made in a hurry. Don't forget to pass around the pretzels and peanuts with this cardplayer's delight.

2 cups orange juice, chilled
2 12-ounce cans ginger ale
1 pint chocolate ice cream
Garnish: Grated orange peel

Divide the orange juice and ginger ale among 6 tall frosted glasses. Stir to combine, then top each with a spoonful of ice cream and a sprinkling of orange peel.

Servings: 6 tall glasses

CRANBERRY SODA

This is a colorful and exciting drink—a great celebration for the end of summer.

2 cups fresh cranberries, washed and stemmed
1 cup water
Pinch of salt
1 cup sugar
1 pint vanilla ice cream
1 quart club soda
Colored straws for stirrers

1. Combine the cranberries, water, salt and sugar in a saucepan. Bring to a boil and reduce heat. Simmer until cranberries burst and are soft. Set aside to cool.

2. When ready to serve, place a spoonful of ice cream in each tall glass. Add 2 or 3 tablespoons of the cranberry mixture, and fill the glass with club soda. Add a straw and stir gently.

Servings: 6 tall glasses

ORANGE ICE CREAM SODA

Brightly colored and delicious. Serve this as an after-school treat or as a dessert.

1 12-ounce can frozen orange juice
   concentrate, thawed
½ cup light cream
1 quart ginger ale
1 pint vanilla ice cream
1 pint orange sherbet

1. Put a heaping tablespoon of orange juice concentrate in each glass.

2. Add 1 tablespoon of light cream and mix well.

3. Stir in ¼ cup of ginger ale, and add 1 scoop each of the ice cream and the sherbet.

4. Fill the glasses with the remaining ginger ale. Stir gently and serve with a straw and a long-handled spoon.

Servings: 6 soda glasses

EGG CREAMS

A New York favorite. You can still create an authentic egg cream drink by using whipped egg whites as they did in the "good old days." The egg whites were blended with chocolate syrup in the bottom of a very tall glass and then seltzer water was added to the mixture. Here is an easier way:

1 to 3 tablespoons chocolate syrup
½ cup cold milk or heavy cream
Seltzer or club soda, chilled

Put the chocolate syrup in the bottom of a tall glass. Add the milk or heavy cream and stir with a spoon. Fill the glass with seltzer or club soda and stir well. Add a straw and slurp away.

Servings: 1

OLD-FASHIONED ROOT BEER FLOAT

There's no trick to it . . . .

Fill a glass three-quarters full with cold root beer. Top with a scoop of vanilla ice cream, and add a long-handled spoon and a straw. (To make it really deluxe, add a bit of whipped cream.)

For something a bit different, try a float using sarsaparilla or chocolate soda.

CHOCOLATE SPECTACULAR

An ice cream soda for all seasons.

3 cups cold milk
1 cup heavy cream
1½ cups chocolate syrup
2 tablespoons sugar
1 teaspoon vanilla extract
1 quart club soda
Garnish: Whipped cream, maraschino cherries, and straws

1. Combine milk, cream, chocolate syrup, sugar, and vanilla in a blender. Blend at medium speed for 30 seconds.

2. Place a few ice cubes in each of 4 glasses, and divide the blender mixture among them. Top each with club soda and stir gently. Add a dollop of whipped cream topped with a maraschino cherry, and insert a straw and a long-handled spoon.

Servings: 4 tall glasses

THE JESSE JAMES

Those he-man poker players will go wild for this one.

2 tablespoons powdered instant coffee
Pinch of salt
¼ cup sugar
1 quart milk
¼ teaspoon peppermint extract
2 pints vanilla ice cream
Garnish: Chocolate shavings or
    maraschino cherries

1. Combine the instant coffee, salt, and sugar in a large pitcher.

2. Add 1 cup of the milk and stir until the coffee and sugar are dissolved.

3. Add the remaining milk and the peppermint flavoring and stir well.

4. Pour into soda glasses, top each with a scoop of ice cream, and some chocolate shavings or a cherry. Add a straw and a long-handled spoon.

Servings: 4 soda glasses

APPLE TREE TEA

Take this along for a tailgate picnic—the wonderful aroma alone will warm you up.

1 quart apple juice or cider
1 quart strong hot tea
Pinch of allspice
Pinch of powdered cloves
Pinch of nutmeg
3 thinly sliced oranges
3 thinly sliced lemons
2 3-inch cinnamon sticks
⅓ cup brown sugar, packed
Garnish: Orange and lemon peel

1. Combine all the ingredients, through the brown sugar, in a large saucepan and bring to a boil. Reduce heat and simmer for 10 minutes.

2. Strain into a thermos or preheated cups. Garnish with orange and lemon peel, if desired.

Servings: 12 cups

BLACKBERRY DANDY

Dungeons & Dragons, Monopoly, and late-night card games will all be a little more exciting with this treat!

1 cup lemonade (made from concentrate)
2 cups canned or frozen blackberries, with juice
1 cup club soda
½ cup sugar
1 quart ginger ale
Garnish: Lemon twists

1. Combine all the ingredients except the ginger ale in a blender, and blend for 20 seconds or until smooth.

2. Put some ice cubes in frosted tankards, and add the blender mixture until they are half filled.

3. Fill tankards with ginger ale, stir, and serve topped with a lemon twist.

Servings: 8 tankards

CRANBERRY JUICE

While it is certainly easier to have quart bottles on hand in your pantry, you can make your own when cranberries are available in the supermarkets and store it in the freezer.

1 pound fresh cranberries, washed and stemmed
2 cups sugar
6 cups water

1. Place the cranberries, sugar, and water in a 2-quart saucepan and bring to a boil. Reduce heat and simmer until the cranberries burst and are soft.

2. Place a sieve over a bowl and line it with cheesecloth. Strain the cranberry juice through the cheesecloth.

3. Cool and serve over ice, or refrigerate and use as needed.

Servings: 4 tall glasses

CRANBERRY JUBILEE PUNCH

Try out a quart of that homemade cranberry juice on some thirsty cheerleaders.

1 quart homemade cranberry juice, chilled (or store-bought cranberry juice cocktail)
2 pints lime sherbert
Garnish: Wafer-thin lime slices

Fill punch cups or paper cups with cranberry juice. Add a heaping spoonful of sherbet, and top with a slice of lime.

Servings: 12 small cups

CURRANT WATER

Raspberry and strawberry water may be made in the same way.

½ pint ripe currants
1 quart water
1 cup sugar
Extra whole berries for garnish

1. Stem the currants, then place them in a medium-size bowl, and crush them slightly by pressing with the back of a wooden spoon. Add just enough water to cover and let them stand for about 1 hour.

2. Strain the currants, reserving the liquid. Wrap the strained currants in a clean dish towel and squeeze it over the bowl of strained liquid. This should give you about 1 cup of juice.

3. Add the quart of water and the sugar. Stir well and strain again, if necessary, this time into a pitcher that can be put on ice until you are ready to serve.

4. Garnish with extra whole currants.

Servings: 6 small glasses

PILGRIM'S CIDER

Throughout the fall season this is a delicious and dependable punch. To save time, make it ahead, then warm it up just before serving. Guests will love it!

2 cups water
½ cup brown sugar, packed
1 teaspoon grated orange peel
1 teaspoon coriander seeds
1 teaspoon allspice
¼ teaspoon nutmeg
2 teaspoons whole cloves
4 3-inch cinnamon sticks
⅓ cup fresh lemon juice
2 quarts apple cider, warmed
Garnish: Extra cinnamon sticks

1. Combine water, sugar, orange peel and spices in a small saucepan. Bring to a boil, reduce heat, and simmer, covered, for 15 minutes.

2. Place a sieve or colander lined with cheesecloth over a large prewarmed punch bowl. Strain the spice mixture through the cheesecloth. Add the lemon juice and apple cider and stir.

3. Serve in punch cups garnished with a cinnamon stick.

Servings: 24 punch cups

ORANGE GROG

Take this in a thermos to a chilly Saturday football game.

2 quarts fresh orange juice
1 cup sugar
3 3-inch cinnamon sticks
20 whole cloves
3 tablespoons grated orange peel

1. Place all the ingredients, through the grated peel, in a large saucepan. Bring to a boil, reduce heat, and simmer for 5 minutes.

2. Strain grog through a colander or sieve into a large pitcher, and then pour it into your thermos.

Servings: 16 mugs

DAPPER APPLE

When apples are plentiful in the fall, enjoy this unusual drink for a change of pace.

2 large apples, cored, peeled, and cut into small pieces
2 cups cold buttermilk
¼ cup sugar
¼ teaspoon cinnamon
Garnish: Grated nutmeg or ground cinnamon

Place the apple pieces, buttermilk, and sugar in a blender and blend for 1 minute or until smooth. Pour into glasses and sprinkle with nutmeg or cinnamon.

Servings: 2 small glasses

BETTY'S MULLED CIDER

My friend Betty serves this rich, aromatic punch at her terrific parties.

5 cups cider
24 whole cloves
4 2-inch cinnamon sticks
4 cups grape juice
½ cup lemon juice
2 quarts ginger ale (not chilled)
3 oranges, sliced thin

1. Place the cider in a large saucepan with the cloves and cinnamon. Bring to a boil and simmer for 5 minutes.

2. Add the grape and lemon juices, stir, and pour into a punch bowl.

3. Pour in the ginger ale and stir gently. Add the orange slices.

Servings: 30 punch cups

THE CHILDREN'S HOUR

This is a really sweet, exceedingly delicious punch appreciated mostly by children. It's perfect for a birthday party or in a separate punch bowl for young guests at a gathering of family and friends.

2 quarts Hawaiian Punch, chilled
2 quarts cranberry juice cocktail, chilled
2 quarts cherry soda, chilled
1 pint strawberry sherbet, softened

Combine the Hawaiian Punch, cranberry juice, and cherry soda in a punch bowl. Add the sherbet and slowly stir to distribute it throughout.

Servings: 50 punch cups

PEACH PUNCH

Warm and tangy for Indian Summer.

1 46-ounce can peach nectar
2 cups fresh orange juice
⅓ cup brown sugar, packed
3 2-inch cinnamon sticks, crumbled
6 whole cloves
2 tablespoons lime juice, fresh if possible
Garnish: Grated orange peel

1. Combine peach nectar, orange juice, and brown sugar in a large saucepan. Bring to a boil, reduce heat, and simmer. Add the spices and stir until the sugar is dissolved, 5 minutes. Add the lime juice and stir.

2. Place a strainer over a prewarmed punch bowl and strain the punch into it.

3. Ladle into punch cups and sprinkle each serving with a bit of orange peel.

Servings: 12 punch cups

WITCHIE'S STEW

A spooky brew—great for Trick-or-Treaters. (To really make it dramatic, just behind the punch bowl set a small container of dry ice with a bit of water added: it'll hiss and steam!)

1 cup orange juice
6 whole cloves
3 cinnamon sticks
3 quarts cold apple cider
2 pints orange sherbet
Garnish: Miniature marshmallows

1. Combine orange juice, cloves, and cinnamon sticks in a small saucepan and heat to boiling. Remove from the heat and set aside to cool.

2. Fill a large punch bowl with the cider. Add the seasoned orange juice and the sherbet. Stir gently.

3. Ladle into small mugs or paper cups and top with mini-marshmallows.

Servings: 24 cups

FISHMONGER'S PUNCH

Fast and easy—serve a batch and chill a batch.

1 quart ginger ale
1 quart pineapple juice
1 16-ounce bottle grape juice
1 quart orange juice
1 quart lemonade (made from concentrate)

Combine all the ingredients in a punch bowl and mix well. Add a large block of ice or several trays of ice cubes.

Servings: 48 punch cups

HAWAIIAN COFFEE PUNCH

Here's another way to use Hawaiian Punch, in a real taste pleaser—for grown-ups this time!

2 cups strong coffee, chilled
2 cups Hawaiian Punch
1 pint vanilla ice cream
1 quart strawberry soda
Garnish: Pineapple cubes

1. Combine half of the coffee, Hawaiian Punch, and ice cream in a blender. Blend at high speed.

2. Place the remaining coffee, Hawaiian Punch, and ice cream in a punch bowl. Add the blender mixture and the strawberry soda. Stir gently.

3. Ladle into punch cups with a pineapple cube in each.

Servings: 18 punch cups

SPARKLING CITRUS PUNCH

Put a winner on the table at the next fraternity or sorority bash.

2 6-ounce cans limeade concentrate, thawed
1 quart unsweetened grapefruit juice
1 teaspoon bitters
1 quart club soda
Garnish: Wafer-thin lime slices

1. Combine the limeade concentrate, juice, and bitters in a large punch bowl and mix well.

2. Just before serving, add some ice cubes and the club soda. Mix thoroughly.

3. Serve in salt-rimmed cups garnished with lime slices.

Servings: 24 punch cups

FAMILY THANKSGIVING PUNCH

The ultimate in color and cranberry flavor, accented with other fruit juices and delicately spiced.

1 quart water
¼ teaspoon grated nutmeg
1 teaspoon whole cloves
1 teaspoon coriander seed
2 3-inch cinnamon sticks
2 quarts cranberry juice cocktail
2 cups pineapple juice
4 cups grapefruit juice
Garnish: 1 cup raisins

1. Combine the water and spices in a large saucepan, bring to a boil, and simmer for 15 minutes.

2. Add the juices and bring just to boiling. Remove from heat.

3. Strain punch through a sieve or colander into a large preheated punch bowl. Place a few raisins in each cup before serving the punch.

Servings: 20 punch cups

SPICE BAG

When you are preparing a warm punch that uses whole spices, make a little bag for the spices—it saves on messy straining. All you need is a little square of cheesecloth, about 5 x 5 inches, and a bit of string. Place the spices in the center of the square, bring all four corners together, and tie. When you are through brewing the hot drink, simply remove the bag and throw it away.

CROCK-POT CRANBERRY

A wassail delicious and fair.

2 cups cranberry juice cocktail
2 quarts apple cider
½ cup sugar
1 orange studded with whole cloves
2 3-inch cinnamon sticks
Garnish: Orange slices or extra
   cinnamon sticks

Combine all the ingredients in a crock-pot and simmer for several hours. Serve in warmed mugs.

Servings: 10 mugs

SPICY HOT CRANBERRY-LEMON PUNCH

Another cranberry concoction to serve at a fall feast.

2 6-ounce cans frozen lemonade,
   slightly thawed
2 cups cranberry juice cocktail
½ teaspoon ground allspice
¼ teaspoon ground cinnamon
Pinch of salt
3 cups water
Garnish: Cinnamon sticks

Place the lemonade, cranberry juice, and the spices with the water in a saucepan. Bring to a boil over medium heat, then lower and simmer for 10 minutes. Serve piping hot in punch cups with a bit of cinnamon stick for garnish.

Servings: 16 punch cups

HOT AND MERRY CRANBERRY

A warm and inviting punch for a harvest table, a teachers' tea, or a Thanksgiving Day feast.

1 quart cranberry-apple drink
2 cups water
1 cup sugar
6 sticks cinnamon
10 whole cloves
Peel of 1 lemon, cut in thin strips
¼ cup fresh lemon juice
Garnish: Apple slices

1. Combine cranberry-apple drink, water, sugar, spices, and lemon peel in a large saucepan. Bring to a boil and simmer for 10 minutes.

2. Place a sieve or colander over a large bowl or pitcher. Strain the cranberry punch through this, and set it aside to cool for 15 minutes.

3. Add the lemon juice and stir. Pour the punch into a punch bowl.

4. Place apple slices in each punch cup before serving the punch.

Servings: 16 punch cups

HOT MOCHA PUNCH

Thanksgiving guests just might stay later for second helpings of pie. If they do, here is a perfect companion. No trouble at all to make—and very good.

1 quart chocolate ice cream
2 quarts hot coffee
Garnish: Grated nutmeg

Place the ice cream in a punch bowl. Pour the hot coffee over it and beat the mixture with a wire whisk until the ice cream is nearly melted. Serve in punch cups with a dash of nutmeg for garnish.

Servings: 16 punch cups

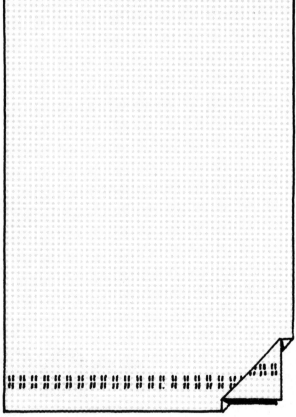

HOT STUFF

Heating your mugs or punch bowl before adding a hot drink helps keep the drink hot and tasty.

❖Rinse them out under hot tap water and dry quickly and thoroughly, then fill.

❖For a large group, put them in the dishwasher on the "dry" cycle, and leave them there until you need them.

❖Put them on an electric hot tray until you are ready to serve.

WINTER WONDER-FULS

Thirsty guests assembled by a warm fireside, shoppers chilled to the bone, carolers bundled for a night of song, wee ones helping to decorate the tree, festive open houses, and holiday dinner parties . . . something for everyone!

There are plenty of hot-drink suggestions here for warming up a blustery winter night or welcoming home cold sledders and skiers.

Nothing is more welcoming than a punch bowl full of frothy, creamy eggnog during this party season. Eggnog keeps well and is wonderful to have on hand in the refrigerator. Also, don't forget Valentine's Day and St. Patrick's Day—wintertime events that call for a special celebratory brew.

LEMON/ TARRAGON GRANITE

Serve this as a refreshing appetizer—excellent with fish or poultry. For sweet granites see page 66.

2 cups water
1 cup fresh lemon juice
¼ cup sugar
1 teaspoon dried tarragon leaves
1 teaspoon grated lemon peel
Few drops yellow food coloring
Garnish: Mint leaves

1. Combine all the ingredients through the tarragon in a large saucepan and bring to a boil. Continue boiling until the quantity is reduced by half.

2. Pour the liquid through a strainer into a cake pan. Mix in the grated lemon peel and food coloring, and set aside to cool. When cool, place in the freezer and freeze uncovered until solid.

3. Remove the pan from the freezer and scoop out the frozen granite with a spatula, dropping the chunks into a large mixing bowl. Beat with an electric mixer until slushy, and then spoon into a large covered container and refreeze.

4. To serve, soften slightly and scoop out portions. Serve in empty lemon shells, if desired, and decorate with mint leaves.

Servings: 6

TOMATO GRANITE

Season this with coriander leaves—an unusual start for a spirited holiday dinner party.

2 cups water
1 cup white vinegar
½ cup fresh coriander leaves, packed
1 14½-ounce can stewed tomatoes
Garnish: Parsley sprigs

1. Combine the water, vinegar, and coriander leaves in a large saucepan, bring to a boil, and continue boiling until the quantity is reduced by half.

2. Pour the reduced mixture through a strainer into a cake pan.

3. Pour the stewed tomatoes into a blender, and blend at medium speed for 1 minute. Stir the tomatoes into the water mixture in the cake pan. When cool, place in the freezer and freeze uncovered until solid.

4. Remove the cake pan from the freezer, and scoop out the frozen granite with a spatula, dropping the chunks into a large mixing bowl. Beat with an electric mixer until slushy. Spoon into a large container and refreeze.

5. To serve, soften slightly and scoop out portions. Serve in hollowed-out tomato halves, if desired, and garnish with parsley.

Servings: 6 punch cups

THE ONLY TOAST YOU'LL NEED

Let's drink to all the joy-filled hours
Grinning babes and dainty flowers
Forget the tears we may have shed
The jobs we've lost, the jerks we've wed.
Look to the stars, look to the sun
Here's to laughter and here's to fun!

ASPARAGUS APPETIZER

Double the quantity for a delicious opener at a small buffet, or for a ladies' luncheon. You can serve it hot or cold.

1 10½-ounce can condensed cream of asparagus soup
1 cup cold milk
¾ teaspoon onion salt
¾ teaspoon celery salt
Juice of half a lemon
Salt and freshly ground pepper to taste
Garnish: Paprika

Combine all the ingredients, through the pepper, in a blender and blend for 1 minute or until smooth. Pour into pretty demitasse cups or crystal-clear punch cups, and give each a dash of paprika.

Servings: 4 small cups

PINK ELEPHANT

These look attractive when served in large brandy snifters—a tasty way to toast the New Year.

1 teaspoon lime juice (fresh or bottled)
1 teaspoon grenadine
1 teaspoon sugar
½ cup bitter lemon
½ cup pink grapefruit juice

1. Mix lime juice, grenadine, and sugar together in a snifter.

2. Add ice cubes, bitter lemon, and grapefruit juice. Stir and serve.

Servings: 1 brandy snifter

GINGER MINT

A quick highball—extra good when served in a frosted glass.

1 whole fresh lime
Ginger ale
Garnish: Several sprigs of fresh mint

Squeeze fresh lime juice into a tall frosted glass. Add some ice cubes and fill with ginger ale. Stir, and add mint.

Servings: 1 tall glass

NONSHRIMP COCKTAIL

Finishing up your Christmas list? This is for you!

¾ cup tomato juice
1 teaspoon horseradish
Dash of Tabasco
Dash of Worcestershire sauce
Dash of lemon juice
Salt and freshly ground pepper to taste
Garnish: Twist of lemon peel

Put all the ingredients, through the salt and pepper, in a short, fat glass and stir briskly. Add some crushed ice and a lemon twist.

Servings: 1

RED HOT GRANNY

Not such a fancy-schmancy appetizer—but easy to make and it inspires appetites for a hearty meal.

3 10½-ounce cans condensed beef broth (bouillon)
1½ cups water
2 teaspoons horseradish
½ teaspoon dill weed
Garnish: Lemon slivers or parsley

Combine all the ingredients, through the dill, in a medium-size saucepan and bring just to a boil. Reduce heat and simmer briefly. Serve in small mugs or punch cups, with a sliver of lemon or a sprig of parsley for garnish.

Servings: 8 small cups

ROOSTER'S PET

Although commercial eggnog is available during the holiday season, it is easy to make your own and great to have ready for unexpected guests—and you don't have to wait for the holidays!

3 cups cold milk
3 eggs
3 tablespoons sugar
1 teaspoon vanilla extract
Pinch of grated nutmeg
Garnish: Extra grated nutmeg

1. Place all the ingredients in a blender and blend for 20 seconds.

2. Pour into a small bowl and sprinkle with nutmeg.

Servings: 8 small punch cups

COFFEE EGGNOG

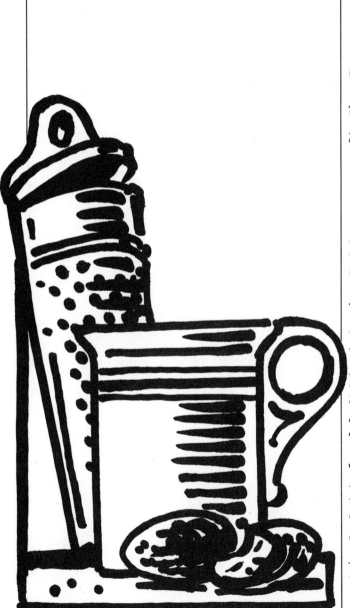

Coffee-flavored eggnog is a real treat and this recipe is flavorful and simple enough to make.

1 quart commercial eggnog
1 quart cold, strong coffee
½ cup sugar
Pinch of grated nutmeg
Garnish: Extra grated nutmeg

1. Place half of the ingredients, through the nutmeg, in a blender and blend for 30 seconds. Pour into a small punch bowl. Repeat with the other half and stir the batches together.

2. Garnish with grated nutmeg.

Servings: 16 punch cups

Note: Another way to make a coffee eggnog is to simply add 6 tablespoons of powdered instant coffee to *Rooster's Pet* and adjust the sugar according to taste.

CARAMEL EGGNOG

A subtle flavor in a creamy eggnog drink.

⅓ cup sugar
1½ cups boiling water
3 eggs, separated
Dash of vanilla extract
1 quart light cream
Pinch of salt
Garnish: Maraschino cherries

1. Place the sugar in a small saucepan over low heat and stir until it forms an amber liquid (caramel).

2. Slowly add the boiling water and stir until the caramel dissolves. Remove from the heat, pour into a small bowl, and chill.

3. Meanwhile, beat the egg yolks until they are thick. Set them aside.

4. Place the egg whites in a separate bowl, add the vanilla, and beat until they are very stiff and form peaks.

5. Just before serving, combine the caramel with the cream in a small punch bowl. Then, gently fold the egg whites into the egg yolks. Carefully stir the eggs into the caramel-cream mixture and add the salt.

6. Serve immediately, in punch cups or old-fashioned glasses garnished with the cherries.

Servings: 6 punch cups

MOCK MOOSE MILK

A warm drink for a cold day. Fill a thermos for skaters, skiers, and sledders.

3 cups milk
3 tablespoons sugar
½ teaspoon almond extract
1 teaspoon rum flavoring

1. In a small, heavy saucepan, scald the milk: heat it just until tiny bubbles form around the edge. Remove from heat.

2. Add the rest of the ingredients to the milk. Stir to blend well.

3. Serve immediately in heated mugs or pour into a thermos to serve later on.

Servings: 3

CARAMEL MILK

This makes a sweet and soothing bedtime drink.

1 cup hot milk
2 tablespoons dark brown sugar
Dash of vanilla extract

Combine all the ingredients in a mug. Stir, and serve warm.

Servings: 1

ORANGE NOG SUPREME

The most exciting and delicious of all the eggnogs—more trouble to concoct, but well worth the effort.

2 quarts orange juice
½ cup fresh lemon juice
6 eggs
¼ cup sugar
¼ teaspoon ground cinnamon
¼ teaspoon ground cloves
¼ teaspoon ground ginger
Pinch of grated nutmeg
1 quart vanilla ice cream
1 quart ginger ale
Garnish: Extra grated nutmeg

1. Place half of the ingredients, through the nutmeg in a blender and blend until smooth. Pour into a large container. Repeat with the other half and combine the two batches. Cover and refrigerate.

2. Meanwhile, place the ice cream and ginger ale in a large punch bowl. Break up the ice cream into chunks. Then, using a hand rotary beater or wire whisk, beat the mixture until it is well blended.

3. Add the refrigerated ingredients and continue beating until all are incorporated.

4. Sprinkle with nutmeg and serve.

Servings: 32 punch cups

YULENOG

Good for caroling parties, when remembering the lyrics is important!

6 eggs, separated
⅓ cup honey (or granulated sugar)
5 cups cold milk
2 tablespoons rum extract
1 teaspoon vanilla extract
1 cup whipped cream
Garnish: Grated nutmeg

1. Beat the egg whites with an electric mixer until soft peaks form.

2. Add the egg yolks and the honey. Continue beating.

3. Slowly add the milk, rum and vanilla extracts, and beat until blended. Chill.

4. Just before serving, fold in the whipped cream and sprinkle with nutmeg.

Servings: 16 punch cups

BANANA EGGNOG

An energy-filled drink for folk who are tired after a New Year's Eve bash.

3 eggs
3 bananas, cut into small pieces
½ pint vanilla ice cream
3½ cups cold milk
Pinch of grated nutmeg
Garnish: Extra grated nutmeg

1. Place the eggs, bananas, ice cream, and 1½ cups of the milk in a blender. Blend at high speed until creamy.

2. Pour the mixture into a small punch bowl and stir in the remaining milk.

3. Sprinkle with grated nutmeg and serve in punch cups.

Servings: 8 small punch cups

COFFEE PUNCH

For a glorious open house—very easy to make and very easy to drink.

4 quarts strong, cold coffee
1 quart light cream
1 tablespoon vanilla extract
1 quart vanilla ice cream, softened
1 cup sugar
Garnish: Whipped cream and shaved chocolate

1. Combine the coffee, cream, and vanilla in a large bowl.

2. Place the ice cream in a second large punch bowl and slowly pour the coffee mixture over it. Stir to blend with a wire whisk, adding the sugar gradually.

3. To serve, ladle the punch into cups and top each with a dollop of whipped cream and a sprinkling of chocolate.

Servings: 32 punch cups

CRIMSON CHRISTMAS PUNCH

This delectable holiday punch speaks for itself—rich in color and easy to make. The trick for elegance lies in the serving.

1 quart cranberry juice cocktail
1 quart red currant juice concentrate
1 quart lemon-lime soda
Ice ring made with lime slices and cherries (see page 8)

Combine the fruit juices in a punch bowl. Just before serving, stir in the lemon-lime soda and add the ice ring.

Servings: 24 punch cups

CANDLELIGHT HOLLY-DAY PUNCH

Hot or cold, this punch tastes best when served by candle-light. For the cold version, make an ice ring with holly leaves (no berries, please) and maraschino cherries.

2 quarts apple cider
1 quart orange juice
Juice of 2 lemons
4 3-inch cinnamon sticks
2 tablespoons whole cloves
1 tablespoon allspice
Pinch of nutmeg
Pinch of ground mace
1 cup honey

Cold: Combine all the ingredients in a large saucepan, stir, and bring to a boil. Reduce the heat and simmer for 10 minutes. Strain the punch into several large pitchers and refrigerate. At serving time, pour into a large punch bowl and add the holly ice ring.

Hot: Combine all the ingredients in a large saucepan, stir, and bring to a boil. Reduce the heat and simmer for 10 minutes. Strain into a prewarmed punch bowl and serve immediately.

Servings: 20 punch cups

MISTLETOE PUNCH

A fast punch for 30 which goes especially well with those holiday fruits, cookies, and candies.

1 6-ounce can frozen lemonade
  concentrate, thawed
1 6-ounce can frozen orange juice
  concentrate, thawed
6 cups water
½ cup grenadine syrup
1 quart ginger ale, chilled
Garnish: Wafer-thin lemon slices and
  maraschino cherries

Combine all the ingredients, through the grenadine, in a punch bowl. Just before serving, add some ice cubes and gently stir in the ginger ale. Put a lemon slice and a cherry in each punch cup, and serve.

Servings: 30 punch cups

THE DRY EDITH

Try this or the *Red Nun* if your stomach feels bloated after a festive holiday party.

1 large glass club soda (with ice)
Large dash of bitters
1 piece lemon rind
Add the bitters to the iced club soda, drop in a healthy chunk of lemon rind and stir.

Servings: 1

RED NUN

1 large glass 7-Up (with ice)
Dash of bitters
Combine the soda with the bitters, and down the hatch.

Servings: 1

AUNT FANNY'S PARTY PUNCH

This punch is proportioned for 70. It is an open house *must.*

1 46-ounce can pineapple juice
1 46-ounce can apricot nectar
1 quart orange juice
2 quarts orange sherbet
2 pints vanilla ice cream
1 10-ounce package frozen strawberries, thawed
2 quarts ginger ale, chilled
Garnish: Pineapple cubes, mint sprigs, and whole strawberries

Combine all the fruit juices in a large punch bowl. Beat the sherbet and ice cream in with a whisk, leaving them in small chunks. Add the strawberries. Gently stir in the ginger ale and place a large piece of ice, or an ice ring, in the bowl. Add garnish (enough so that your guests will scoop up a bit with each serving).

Servings: 70 punch cups

ESKIMO PUNCH

A coldy but goody. Create a decorative garnish for these by alternating pineapple cubes and maraschino cherries on a toothpick and serving one with each cup.

3 cups apricot nectar
3 cups pineapple juice
1 quart orange juice
1 quart 7-Up
1 quart ginger ale or club soda
Garnish: Fruit (see above)

Combine all the juices in a punch bowl and stir. Add some ice cubes and gently mix in the soda. Serve with fruit kabob garnishes.

Servings: 36 punch cups

GRAPE FRAPPE

A drink rich in color and flavor makes a welcome change at a small winter get-together.

2 cups grape juice
2 tablespoons fresh lemon juice
½ cup sugar
2 cups water
2 cups light cream
1 pint grape ice cream or sherbet
Garnish: 8 wafer-thin lemon slices

1. Place the grape juice, lemon juice, and sugar in a large pitcher and stir.

2. Gradually add the water and light cream, stirring with each addition.

3. Put half of the mixture in a blender and add the ice cream. Blend for 1 minute.

4. Pour blender mixture into the pitcher and combine with the pitcher mixture.

5. Serve in tall glasses over cracked ice. Garnish each serving with a lemon slice.

Servings: 8 tall glasses

PURPLE PASSION

This is a delicious and inexpensive way to serve the multitudes—those thirsty square-dancers, for instance.

1 ice ring (see page 8)
4 quarts grape juice
1 quart lemon juice (can be made from concentrate)
1 quart pineapple juice
9 quarts club soda
4 cups sugar, dissolved in 2 cups hot tap water
Garnish: Maraschino cherries

1. Place the ice ring in a metal washtub or other container.

2. Add the rest of the ingredients to the tub and stir gently to mix.

3. Place a maraschino cherry in the bottom of each punch cup and serve.

Servings: 140 punch cups

HOT SPICED GRAPE JUICE

This can be made ahead and kept on hand in your crock pot as a welcoming hot drink for New Year's Eve guests.

1 quart grape juice
1 quart cranberry juice cocktail
4 whole cloves
1 large stick cinnamon
3 whole allspice
½ cup brown sugar, packed
⅓ cup white sugar

1. Place all the ingredients in a medium-size saucepan and stir until they are well mixed.

2. Cook over low heat until the sugar is dissolved.

3. Strain, and serve in mugs.

Servings: 10 mugs

STUPID CUPID

A fabulous drink for an after-school Valentine's Day party.

2 cups frozen strawberries, thawed
    and crushed
1 cup orange juice
⅓ cup lemon juice
1 quart cold milk
Garnish: Maraschino cherries

1. Place all the ingredients in a blender and blend at medium speed for 1 minute.

2. Pour the mixture into a pitcher, cover, and refrigerate until well chilled.

3. Serve in frosted glasses topped with a cherry.

Servings: 6 tall glasses

SWEETHEART BERRY-BERRY

Enough for a couple of romantic Valentines.

1 pint raspberry sherbet
2 cups cold milk

Place the ingredients in a blender and blend on high speed for 15 seconds. Serve in tall glasses.

Servings: 2 tall glasses

SHILLELAGH SIP

For a St. Patrick's Day party…

Green maraschino-cherry ice ring (see page 8)
2 quarts limeade, made from concentrate
1 quart lemon-lime soda

1. Make an ice ring using green maraschino cherry liquid, cherries, and water. Keep in freezer until ready.

2. Place the limeade and lemon-lime soda in a punch bowl large enough to hold the punch plus the ice ring. Stir.

3. Immediately before serving, carefully place the ice ring in the punch bowl.

Servings: 16 small punch cups

SWEET SUE

This drink will slip down along with chips and dips and midnight sandwiches.

1 quart cranberry juice cocktail
1 quart 7-Up
Juice of 1 lime
½ cup sugar
Garnish: 8 wafer-thin lime slices

1. Place all the ingredients in a large pitcher and stir until they are well mixed.

2. Serve over ice in tall glasses, and garnish each with a lime slice.

Servings: 8 tall glasses

LIME TIME

Something cool and green for St. Patrick's Day. Good for adults and children alike.

Large cake of ice
2 quarts pineapple juice
1 cup sugar syrup (see page 62)
1 quart lemon-lime soda
1 quart lime sherbet, softened
Garnish: Green maraschino cherries or
   wafer-thin lime slices

1. Place the ice in a large punch bowl, then add the pineapple juice and the syrup. Gently stir to blend well.

2. Add the lemon-lime soda and the sherbet. Slowly stir the sherbet into the punch with a whisk and blend well.

3. Garnish the punch bowl with cherries or lime slices, and serve.

Servings: 32 punch cups

FESTIVE MOCHA

Festivities can begin or end with a cup of unusually delicious coffee.

3 cups strong, cold coffee
1 pint coffee ice cream
Dash of vanilla extract
4 tablespoons chocolate syrup

Combine all the ingredients in a blender and blend until smooth. Serve in fancy goblets.

Servings: 4 goblets (or 8 punch cups)

MOCHA MIA

Easy and delicious for an intimate moment by the fireside . . .

1 square unsweetened chocolate, coarsely chopped
¼ cup boiling water
1 tablespoon instant coffee
1 tablespoon sugar
1½ cups milk
Garnish: Whipped cream and chocolate shavings

1. Place all the ingredients, through the milk, in a blender and blend at top speed for 20 seconds.

2. Pour into 2 tall glasses and top with a dollop of whipped cream and some chocolate shavings.

Servings: 2 tall glasses

QUICK MOCHA-CAPPUCCINO

This is excellent as an after-dinner drink, as well as a warm welcome home for winter athletes.

2 envelopes cocoa mix (2-ounce size)
3 heaping tablespoons powdered instant coffee
1 cup hot heavy cream
Pinch of ground cinnamon
3 cups boiling water
Garnish: Extra ground cinnamon

1. Place the cocoa, coffee, cream and cinnamon in a blender and blend until frothy.

2. Fill coffee cups two-thirds full with water and add the hot-cream froth. Stir, and sprinkle with extra cinnamon.

Servings: 8

CHOCOLATE ESPRESSO

Here's an opportunity to use those delicate demitasse cups.

½ cup heavy cream
1 tablespoon sugar
Dash of vanilla extract
½ teaspoon grated orange peel
4 tablespoons instant espresso coffee
1 cup boiling water
1 cup strong hot chocolate
Garnish: Grated nutmeg

1. Whip the cream together with the sugar and vanilla. Fold in the grated orange peel. Set aside.

2. Combine the espresso, hot chocolate, and boiling water in a glass or ceramic coffee pot and stir.

3. Pour the coffee into demitasse cups and top each one with a spoonful of the whipped cream. Garnish with a sprinkling of nutmeg.

Servings: 6 demitasse cups

FRENCH CHOCOLATE

This delicate chocolate will fuel up the tree trimmers. And remember to leave a cup for Santa!

3 squares unsweetened chocolate
¾ cup water
¾ cup sugar
Pinch of salt
½ cup heavy cream, whipped
1 quart milk, heated but not boiling
Garnish: Extra whipped cream and
  chocolate shavings

1. Combine chocolate and water in a small saucepan. Cook over low heat, stirring constantly, until the chocolate is melted.

2. Add the sugar and salt, and boil gently for 3 minutes, stirring constantly.

3. Remove from the heat and fold in the whipped cream.

4. Put 1 tablespoon of this chocolate mixture in each cup, and add hot milk to fill and stir. Top with a spoonful of whipped cream and chocolate.

Servings: 6 coffee cups

DRINKS FOR ALL OCCASIONS

DIET DRINKS

HOLIDAY DRINKS

DRINKS FOR A CROWD

CHILDREN'S FAVORITES

INDEX